The Professional Development of School Administrators

The Professional Development of School Administrators:

Preservice, Induction, and Inservice Applications

JOHN C. DARESH
University of Northern Colorado, Greeley

MARSHA A. PLAYKO
Ohio LEAD Center, Westerville

ALLYN AND BACON
Boston   London   Toronto   Sydney   Tokyo   Singapore

Copyright © 1992 by Allyn and Bacon
A Division of Simon & Schuster, Inc.
160 Gould Street
Needham Heights, Massachusetts 02194

Library of Congress Cataloging-in-Publication Data

Daresh, John C.
    The professional development of school administrators :
preservice, induction, and inservice applications / John C. Daresh,
Marsha A. Playko.
        p.   cm.
    Includes bibliographical references and index.
    ISBN 0-205-13201-4
    1. School administrators—Training of—United States.   2. School
administrators—In-service training—United States.   I. Playko,
Marsha A., 1950–   . II. Title.
LB1738.5.D37   1992
371.2'01—dc20   91-24753
                                                             CIP

Printed in the United States of America

10   9   8   7   6   5   4   3   2   1   95   94   93   92   91

To our families . . .
Bridget and Stephanie
and
Kelly, Nick, Mark, and Rich

Contents

Preface

In recent years, researchers have pinpointed effective leadership of organizations as perhaps the single most important determinant of success. This has been highlighted in analyses of school practices which show that the quality of the leadership demonstrated by principals, superintendents, and other administrators has a major impact on the overall effectiveness of schools and districts. Despite these observations, however, there has been a remarkable lack of focused attention to examining how people become school leaders or how they are supported once they assume those roles.

We have prepared this book as a response to this need to understand more completely how leadership of schools can be improved through professional development. When we use that term, we are looking at three distinct phases of a person's career: preservice preparation, induction (or the process of first coming "on board"), and continuing inservice education. Too often, there is an assumption that good school leaders simply happen and, once they do, continue to be effective for many years, until they retire. In this book we take a view that leaders are not the product of such a magical process. It takes hard work to learn the art, science, and craft of educational administration, and it takes a similar amount of hard work to keep needed leadership skills well tuned over time.

We organize our vision of professional development for school leaders around several important issues. First, we consider a model that we believe is useful in terms of understanding three different ways in which people can learn about leadership: academic preparation, field-based learning, and professional formation. The last of these is a perspective rarely considered in most discussions of how people learn about administration. Yet considerable research suggests that what we describe as the formation process may indeed be the most crucial part of how effective leaders are first prepared.

We use this model of professional development to organize our discussions of a number of concepts and practices related to the preservice preparation, induction, and ongoing inservice education of educational leaders. Included is material that looks at mentoring programs, the relationship between research on teacher preparation and administrator development, studies of beginning administrators, and alternative models that may be used in the delivery of effective administrator inservice. Included throughout are numerous examples of effective practices and procedures that have addressed all of these issues.

Our fundamental assumptions throughout this book, we believe, are clear. We believe that administrators of schools are important people, and that they are indeed "worth it" when thinking about opportunities for professional development. We also believe that the investment of time and other resources in the enhancement of leadership skills will have a powerful impact on the ultimate quality of education in this nation. In short, we assume that professional development for school leaders is not a frill, to be added on when districts find a few extra dollars in their budgets. To the contrary, we think that spending money on the improvement of leadership is a sound decision that will have significant future organizational payoffs.

Finally, we believe that the process of effective professional development for school leaders is something that demands serious planning and attention. It does not simply "happen" without any thought on the part of those responsible for directing such an effort. We believe that the material presented in this book will be an important and useful guide for those who would take on the critical duty of helping leaders to grow.

*The Professional
Development of
School Administrators*

CHAPTER ONE

The Preparation of American School Administrators: What the Past Tells the Future

People who are aware of the structure of public education in the United States know that there is something unique about the way we do things in this country. For example, we do not have a national education mandate. In the United States, public education is said to be a reflection of the concept of plenary power at the state level of governance. Because the United States Constitution contains no explicit statement of the federal government's role regarding public education, it has been implied that any activity in this area is part of the responsibilities of the individual states. As a result, we actually have fifty-one (including the District of Columbia) separate school systems in the United States. And because the value of "local control" is so deeply ingrained in the minds of most Americans, we have many more than fifty-one school districts because most states have several systems. Technically, we have over 15,000 systems of public education at work in this country!

Not surprisingly, there are considerably more similarities than dissimilarities among these different systems. A visitor to a classroom in South Carolina will find the same sorts of things a person would see in schools in Ohio or Colorado. To be sure, there are certainly distinctions between the schools that serve wealthy condominium owners in Hilton Head, farmers in central Ohio, or residents of the inner city of Denver. But for the most part, American schools look alike. Not everyone is convinced that this is a good thing. In recent years, we have seen forceful calls for restructuring (not simply reforming) schools, and for emphasizing differences among educational systems, as supported by such schemes as voucher plans and school choice proposals.

At the outset of this book we make a few assumptions about the nature of schooling and how it may or may not change in the United States in the foreseeable future. First, we believe there will always be people who serve as leaders of schools, regardless of any restructure or reform. The people who are leaders may not always be limited to those who serve as formal school administrators. In fact, we seriously doubt that there will ever be a day when leadership of schools is seen as something that resides solely in the administrator's office. But we also believe that individuals will emerge to give direction to educational organizations. When they do, they need support as well as opportunities for professional development, because, as leaders go, so go their organizations.

We also believe that educational leadership is important and that attention needs to be directed to finding ways to help people who take on such positions. Professional development for school leaders, whether the leaders are administrators or not, is something that deserves attention by researchers and practitioners alike. Further, we assume that professional development for school administrators and other educational leaders is a reasonable target for restructuring and reform proposals.

Finally, we believe that whatever might be proposed in the area of professional development would be more effective if those responsible for its improvement were sensitive to the history of educational administration in this country. Formal administration of schools is a relatively new phenomenon; we do not have a long tradition to tell us how people are "supposed" to behave in leadership roles. Yet we do have enough of a history in our field to suggest that school administrators have been expected to play out a wide array of duties in the past, and that an awareness of these former images of leadership may be crucial to developing an appreciation of where the field may go in the future. And the future of administrative and leadership practice related to schools will likely give us some direction concerning where we may go with our approaches to professional development.

In this chapter, we will carry out this third theme by looking at some of the ways in which administration and leadership of schools have been conceptualized in the past, and how they are currently being described in the literature. Based on what the past and present tell us, we will then present a model for the restructuring of professional development that may serve to make school leaders more sensitive to present realities while preparing to meet future challenges.

Historical Trends in Educational Administration

In this section, we consider three alternative historical perspectives on the world of educational administration and leadership. Each of these views is important because it represents not only a time frame, but, more important, a philosophical approach to the ways in which schools should operate. It is our view that the three views also offer us some important insights into the ways in which professional development might be offered for those who serve in leadership roles.

Perspective 1: Scientific Approaches to Administration

From approximately the end of the Civil War until soon after World War I (around 1920), there was tremendous growth in formal educational systems in this country. In addition, individual schools became larger and more complex. The role of the professional educational administrator was born in many school districts in the country as it was recognized that managing a school was more difficult and time-consuming than something that could be done on a part-time basis by a lead ("principal") teacher.

Teaching procedures and educational practices in general were greatly influenced by experts whose interest was primarily the improvement of organizational efficiency. Much of what they believed was affected by the views of various writers on corporation management, particularly Frederick W. Taylor (1916), whose "scientific management principles" were advocated as the way to ensure good practice in industrial organizations. A review of Taylor's major tenets provides a context for our discussion of this first formal period of administrative thought and practice in U.S. schools. The essential points of Taylor's views include the following:

1. *Time-study principle:* All productive effort should be measured by accurate time study and a standard time established for all work done in the shop.

2. *Piece-rate principle:* Wages should be proportional to output and their rates based on the standards determined by time study. As a corollary, a worker should be given the highest grade of work of which he is capable.

3. *Separation-of-planning-from-performance principle:* Management should take over from workers the responsibility for planning the work and making the performance physically possible. Planning should be based on time studies and other data related to production, which are scientifically determined and systematically classified; it should be facilitated by standardization of tools, implements, and methods.

4. *Scientific-methods-of-work principle:* Management should take over from workers the responsibility for their methods of work, determine scientifically the best methods, and train workers accordingly.

5. *Management-control principle:* Managers should be trained and taught to apply scientific principles of management and control (such as management by exception and comparison with validated production standards).

6. *Functional principle:* The strict application of military principles should be reconsidered and the industrial organization should be so designed that it best serves the purpose of improving coordination of activities among the specialists (Villers, 1960, p. 78).

These principles of scientific management imply that certain features of organizational life are so predictable that specific laws can be formulated to guide behavior in virtually every circumstance, and that outcomes are also highly predictable in organizational settings. They formed the basis for much of the scholarship related to educational administration during the era. George Strayer and Ellwood P. Cubberley, for example, became highly influential voices in the literature associated with educational leadership (Culbertson, 1988). The belief reigned that behavioral formulas, when faithfully followed, would necessarily and automatically lead to predictable outcomes and products.

This view of administration strongly suggests that there is a single "right way" of doing things in education, and that once this path is identified, it is the administrator's responsibility to ensure that teachers know and follow it. The administrator is also charged with the responsibility of *planning*—that is, of finding the most efficient and economical ways to attain organizational goals.

Assumptions of Scientific Management

1. *Great faith was placed in educational "laws."* Many educators sincerely believed that scientific research would provide the answer to virtually any problem. Organizations throughout society were awakening to the possibility that rules and principles could be established to guide practice. School administrators in particular were open to this line of thinking, because at this time schools were emerging from over two centuries of rather confused development. The notion that the educational practices of the past could be understood and even improved upon if some key "facts" and laws were learned was indeed tempting.

The outcome of this view was that, increasingly, the educational administrator became a *quality control reviewer* who checked to see if employees conformed to procedures: The administrator's job was to make sure that the "scientific" rules of schooling were being followed. Thus, the emphasis was on the maintenance of acceptable teaching behaviors, and particularly on ensuring that these were carried out efficiently.

2. *Administrators would determine the proper methods of doing things.* This "scientific" approach to administration emphasized a top-down orientation to defining and communicating information concerning school practices. The administrative personnel of a school or district were viewed as the legitimate experts in the field of education, to the extent that such experts could reasonably be expected to define precisely what constituted proper performance. Scientific management principles urging separation of management from employee control made unthinkable the possibility that teachers would work together to influence or define organizational practices. Quite simply, teachers were viewed as the implementors of administrators' policies.

The overriding aim of educational administration as it was practiced during this era was to make certain that what occurred in schools was as "professionally efficient" as possible at all times. Professional efficiency was narrowly defined as competence in such things as self-analysis, self-criticism, and self-improvement—at least in terms of teachers' abilities to conform to stated standards of performance Those standards were always determined at higher levels of the school district organization and then transmitted to the teachers. A primary activity of administrators, then, was to provide either commendations or condemnations to staff. Compromises between these two extremes were not possible.

Implications for Professional Development

Adherence to the assumptions and beliefs of the scientific management perspective for educational administrators calls for certain approaches to be taken relative to the three phases of professional development: preservice preparation, induction, and ongoing inservice education.

In the area of preservice preparation, acceptance of the scientific management perspective suggests that the predominant approach to learning would have involved a good deal of one-way communication from those who possess the "scientific facts" of how to administer schools to those who will serve as administrators in the future. The content of preservice programs would include mostly a collection of facts that describe the "one right way" to do certain things. Books would contain prescriptions for "how to" lead schools: how to finance schools, how to evaluate staff, how to design curriculum, and so forth.

Induction programs, at least in a formal sense, would probably be nonexistent because the assumption was made that people in administrative positions had learned the "facts" in preservice programs, and that they had little more that needed to be learned when they first took a job. If any attention were to be paid to the concerns of beginning administrators, it might simply be directed toward providing more precise definitions to "correct" ways of doing things in a particular school system. As a result, induction might be more properly referred to as orientation.

Finally, inservice education for practitioners who espoused the tenet of scientific management would tend to be devoted to providing assistance to people to learn better (more efficient) ways to carry out the duties that were identified as "effective" during the preservice preparation phase of development. Inservice programs would involve helping practicing administrators learn the most expeditious way to carry out the skills that were taught to them earlier in their careers.

The overriding motto of professional development from the perspective of scientific management might be something like, "There's a right way—and only one right way—to do everything." Professional development consists of teaching people to do things that right way. If these descriptions of professional development sound familiar, it may be due to the fact that the prevailing perspective or philosophical orientation followed for many years has been this approach. Traditional university preservice preparation programs, state certification requirements for administrators, district job descriptions, and inservice programs offered by professional associations tend to suggest that there exists a widely held set of common understandings of the right and wrong ways to administer schools.

Perspective 2: Human Relations Approaches to Administration

One consequence of the "scientific" era of administration was the tendency to value organizational goals more than the interests and needs of the people who worked in the organization. Scientific management often emphasized the notion that all organizational components—employees included—were best understood as replacement parts: "One teacher is just as good as another" could have been the motto of the time. Predictably, a vigorous reactive movement eventually emerged. In the "human relations" era, from approximately 1920 to 1960, an administrative philosophy emerged that placed primary emphasis on developing the individuals who worked in schools and on satisfying their personal interests. Widespread support developed for cooperative group efforts as both an end and a means for change in schools.

What is remarkable about this perspective on administration is the shift in emphasis toward allowing employees to work together to define organizational goals and to create appropriate activities to meet those goals. The top-down emphasis of administrative control has given way to a more democratic process.

There is a great difference between the perspective of this *human development* era of administration and those of the *scientific* era. In the first two centuries of American education, very little concern was expressed about the individual needs of teachers and others in school systems. In the human relations view, however, we find little or no concern for the priorities and needs of the organization.

Assumptions of Human Relations

1. *If people are happy, they will be productive.* This is the fundamental premise of this era, and it is the key ingredient of any approach to managerial practice that endorses the fulfillment of human needs. If we truly believe that happy employees will be better, more effective employees, then the primary task for administrators must be to focus on whatever they determine are the needs

and interests of the workers. Educational administrators must then spend a good deal of time seeking input from teachers and staff members concerning working conditions and other issues related to the quality of life in the organization. Human relations administrators frequently go out of their way to make workers more comfortable.

2. *The improvement of the psychosocial climate of the school is a legitimate concern of administrators.* The human relations movement, which emerged quite forcefully during the 1920s and 1930s, was heavily influenced by the research and theory bases that were increasingly popular in the social sciences. Gestalt psychology and other views that emphasized the need for organizational process development had a strong impact on the prevailing notions of administration. The result of this psychological "intrusion" into administrative practice, however, was not simply that a particular perspective was considered more valid than others. Rather, the overall tenor of administration was altered; it became acceptable for educational leaders to expend energy toward trying to change the "feel" of an organization. Previously, only the measurable outcomes of organizations were considered to be the legitimate concerns of administrators.

Implications for Professional Development

The preservice preparation of school administrators that is influenced by the human relations perspective would give strong emphasis to the development of the interpersonal skills of future leaders. Considerable time would be spent in promoting group process and individual skills in dealing with "people issues." Less time would be devoted to learning the facts and specific skills that were the centerpiece of scientific management programs.

Efforts to provide for the induction of new administrators would focus almost exclusively on the personal needs of the beginner. There would be great concern for the psychological health and welfare of the person coming "on board" for the first time. Little attention would be paid to the acquisition of specific pieces of job-related knowledge. The crucial thing would be making a newcomer feel comfortable.

Inservice education would, in a sense, simply be a continuation of the person-oriented emphasis seen during induction. Learning activities for practitioners would focus almost exclusively on providing for individual growth by participants. Thus, inservice would be devoted to programs designed to help individuals become more satisfied as people rather than focusing on increasing skills related to job performance.

Perspective 3: Human Resource Development Approaches

The predominant perspective on organizations today is reflected in human resource development. This view has incorporated the basic assumption of human relations management (namely, that people in an organization hold the key to more effective management) into a somewhat different approach.

Human resource development suggests that the most important activity of an administrator is to help people within an organization—its "human resources"—become as skillful and effective as possible. The organization will be improved because its most important features—its employees—will be more effective.

There is a good deal of overlap between human relations and human resource development. Both approaches place tremendous emphasis on the needs of the people who work in an organization, and both views hold that organizational effectiveness is a desirable outcome of the intervention by an administrator. In addition, both views suggest that the key to organizational effectiveness is the extent to which workers can feel satisfied with their jobs.

But some important differences keep human resource development from being a mere rehash of the earlier concept. Human relations advocates believed that emphasizing the happiness of an organization's employees would almost automatically guarantee that those employees would work harder, thereby increasing the overall effectiveness and productivity of the organization. The principal duty of the educational administrator, then, would be to make certain that the conditions of employment guaranteed that workers would be content and satisfied with the workplace, and would therefore want to work much harder in the future. By contrast, the human resource development approach advocates that employees will be happier, more satisfied, and ultimately more productive only if they are first satisfied through working in a productive organization.

Proponents of human resource development criticize the earlier human relations perspective as highly manipulative because of its assumption that an administrator, by being nice to employees, can make them "buy into" organizational goals without hesitation.

Human relations advocates, for their part, believe that, because ot its emphasis on organizational productivity, human resource development is but a thinly disguised return to scientific managment. The real distinction seems to be more subtle. In human relations administration, the desire is to satisfy people's needs as an immediate goal and outcome; organizational effectiveness is a by-product. Such an approach shows more immediate results; people tend to be more comfortable in a human relations environment. The human resource development advocates, however, claim that people will *eventually* be happy if the organization is productive, even though their immediate impression may be that the supervisor is ignoring individual needs. Meeting the concerns of employees is a long-term goal for human resource administrators, who believe that immediate energy needs to be directed toward organizational effectiveness.

Assumptions of Human Resource Development

1. *The most important concern of the educational administrator is the improvement of organizational effectiveness.* There is no compromise on this point. The human resource development perspective holds the administrator fully accountable for bringing about more productive, efficient, and effective organizations. Things need to get done, and the administrator is the person who is supposed to provide direction. In this way, there is the same strong attention paid to the importance of organizational goals present in the scientific management perspective. The major difference here is that, unlike the scientific view, there is no assumption of a set of operating rules, or laws, that are likely to "guarantee" desirable organizational outcomes. Human resource development suggests that it is the responsibility of the administrator to work with and through others to create the conditions that will promote greater effectiveness. The top-down orientation of the past is absent in this approach to management. And that single issue differentiates human resource development greatly from scientific management.

2. *Happy employees are productive employees if they work in a productive place.* This twist of the motto associated with human relations management points clearly to the differing perspectives of the two schools of thought. Human relations administrators look at the need to satisfy employees as a direct responsibility; human resource administrators look to the satisfaction of employees as a desirable and legitimate outcome of their work, but in an indirect fashion. People are happy when the organization in which they

work is productive. The administrator who espouses the concept of human resource development becomes primarily interested in bringing about greater organizational effectiveness, thereby creating a setting in which employees can feel satisfied through their association with productivity. In many ways, then, human resource development is an outcome of the human relations movement. The key distinction is in the emphasis selected by the administrator.

Implications for Professional Development

Human resource development would likely influence preservice preparation by placing great emphasis on helping future leaders develop a personalized vision of organizational effectiveness so that they will be able to provide guidance to their future institutions. At the same time, a strong value present in such programs would be one that endorses the importance of the individuals who work in an organization. There would be an effort to blend a focus on organizational outcomes with an appreciation of the people who make up the organization.

Induction programs would emphasize a continuation of learning the same perspectives gained during the preservice phase. Here, the novice administrator would gain further insights into the practicality of the vision for organizational effectiveness developed during preservice. The beginning leader would expend a considerable amount of effort to learn how to work effectively with staff in developing a shared vision of school effectiveness and productivity. This could be a very difficult time for a new administrator who subscribes to human resource development because, at first, teachers might find the emphasis on organizational outcomes to be an approach devoid of any appreciation of their human needs.

Inservice education would consist of helping practicing administrators refine their ability to work with and through people to achieve organizational effectiveness—the goals of human resource development. Inservice might include opportunities for experienced school leaders to enhance skills needed to communicate with staff, or to involve teachers and others more productively in decision making related to the articulation of school goals.

It is likely that all three historical perspectives continue to exist in American school systems. Although one of the approaches may be closest to our own personal set of values related to effective educational management, the important thing to note is that individuals representing all three views are in leadership positions in schools. Approaches to professional development available to people who espouse these various perspectives need to be well designed so that leaders can be prepared effectively for future positions, brought on board successfully, and given ongoing support that allows them to serve the needs of students.

The Present Scene

Regardless of the orientation embraced regarding proper goals and functions of administration, there currently exists a view that school administrators are not doing their jobs in an effective and efficient way. This observation suggests that school administrators are indeed important people when it comes to assessing who is primarily responsible for making schools more productive. It is apparent that administrators are very influential. Further, critics of what is now taking place in schools lay the blame at the feet of school leaders. The recognition of importance is equal to the designation of culpability.

   In response to the criticism of school leadership, the University Council for Educational Administration (UCEA), a consortium of fifty large, doctorate-granting institutions across the United States and Canada, with programs designed to prepare future educational administrators, chartered an effort to review the nature of administrative training at the preservice level. In 1987 the Report of the National Commission on Excellence in Educational Administration was published under the title *Leaders for Tomorrow's Schools: The Report of the National Commission* (Griffiths, Stout, & Forsyth, 1988). Although it has been criticized by many who believed its recommendations not to be forceful or imaginative enough to suggest the type of sweeping changes needed to bring about meaningful improvement, the report contained a clear call for certain modifications and improvements to be made in the ways in which individuals are prepared to assume positions of leadership in schools. We select two of the recommendations made in the report for particular emphasis. First, the report suggested that greater attention be placed on discovering ways in which universities and local education agencies might collaborate more effectively in the preparation of educational administrators. The historic pattern of universities assuming total, or at least the major, control over the preservice instructional content, and the view that school systems are to be passive receivers of people trained according to this pattern, is described as no longer valid. Preparing individuals for future administrative responsibilities has been described as something that needs to be mutually shared by all those who would be identified as legitimate stakeholders in the development of educational leadership.

The second recommendation is that administrative preparation programs must include more opportunities for "clinical" approaches to learning as part of the normal ongoing activities of preservice training. The assumption that a period of "learning by doing" before a person moves into a professional role for the first time is alive and well in the field of administrator preparation. The belief that the preparation of educational personnel must include some practical learning experiences comes from a long historical and philosophical tradition in U.S. education, a tradition dating to the writing of John Dewey (1938). The critical issue here, however, is that the assumptions of the value of field-based learning have rarely been tested, and there is no solid, identified comprehensive theory that guides the use of practica. Despite these limitations, however, the view is present today that people will be better future teachers, counselors, or administrators if they have a time to engage in these roles before taking their first full-time jobs.

In this section, the status of administrator preparation is examined to determine the extent to which the vision of potential ways of improving the preparation of administrators, as suggested through many reform proposals, has been realized. An estimate will be provided of the probability that two major recommendations from the National Commission on Excellence will be addressed. These two recommendations are (1) an increase in efforts to find collaboration and (2) an additional emphasis on clinical preparation. Second, a different conceptualization of the ways in which educational administrators might be prepared is provided.

Attempts to Find Collaboration

The suggestion of the National Commission that the preparation of educational administrators must be the product of alliances formed between universities and local educational agencies appears at first to make good sense. But is there a probability that the type of true collaboration envisioned in this proposal might be found? Certain constraints to true collaboration need to be addressed. Neale, Bailey, and Ross (1981) identified these barriers as (1) institutional territoriality, (2) absence of partner parity, and (3) lack of staff time.

Institutional Territoriality

Each member of a collaborative arrangement has certain institutional loyalties and self-interests that demand attention. These loyalties serve, in large measure, as important indicators of the identity of an organization. In the professional development of school administrators, the members of the collaborative arrangement typically are the university, with its need to generate courses and credit hours, and the local school district, with its need to guarantee that administrative personnel will demonstrate skill in implementing stated local policies and procedures. This typically leads to scenarios in which universities are reluctant to "give up" any training activities to local schools because of the fear that doing so will rob the campus of students needed to fill the lecture halls and fuel the credit hour–driven process. Local school systems, on the other hand, distrust their university colleagues' ability to prepare and support individuals who will successfully defend and understand local policies and priorities. In addition, local education agencies often simply see the professional development of school administrators, particularly at the preservice level, to be the responsibility of universities.

Before the dream of the National Commission regarding collaboration might be achieved, then, strategies must be discovered to reduce the negative effects of institutional territoriality, which has traditionally served to block mutual efforts. Universities need to share their traditional turf regarding training, and local educational agencies need to increase their levels of trust regarding the efforts of university programs. One way of doing this might be for local schools to examine more critically their expectations concerning the roles of administrators. Teachers and other school staff members need to articulate more precisely their own conceptions of good leadership. No one, either in the university or in any other organization, can be expected to prepare and support people for jobs that are, at best, vaguely defined.

Absence of Partner Parity

Neale, Bailey, and Ross defined parity as "the state or condition being the same in power, value, or rank" (1981, p. 45). Although parity is a commendable goal, evidence suggests that strong imbalances have existed in the power relationships found between universities and local educational agencies, and that these have served as barriers to true collaboration. Universities and local school systems have long controlled the licensing and certification processes found in most states. Before true collaboration might ever occur, competition resulting from a lack of balance of power must be resolved so that universities, local school systems, and other partners involved in the professional development of administrators can appreciate the unique potential inherent in supporting leadership development. The conceptual model introduced later in this chapter represents an attempt to identify the special contributions of the various actors involved in administrator preparation.

Staff Time for Collaboration

Maintaining meaningful intraorganizational linkage requires a considerable investment of time and energy on the part of the people within an institution. The reward systems of both major partners in the professional development of school administrators, namely universities and local school systems, do little to reinforce the value of developing ongoing sharing. In most settings, university professors are rewarded (through the granting of academic tenure, promotions, and merit pay increases) for carrying out research, publishing, and, to a lesser extent, teaching their campus-based classes and engaging in university governance activities. They are *not* traditionally recognized for their efforts to develop collaborative partnerships with local school systems. Further, local school personnel are paid to teach children or administer schools, not to foster mutually supportive arrangements with their colleagues at the university. Time is rarely made available to local school staff who wish to engage in university training programs, at least without the loss of a considerable amount of personal pay and removal from important instructional duties.

Collaboration will not result unless clear and consistent signals are provided by all potential partners to the effect that efforts to work with others will be openly valued and rewarded, both financially and with sufficient time.

Attempts to Increase Clinical Preparation

The second major theme found in the recommendations of the National Commission for improving the professional development of administrators is that more attention must be paid to increasing opportunities for clinical preparation. The assumption is that one learns by doing, and that people will be best prepared to serve as educational administrators if they are able to participate in hands-

on activities that will enable them to play the part of the administrator before taking on that role in real life for the first time.

We address the issue of increasing the opportunities for people
to learning through experience more completely in Chapter 3. At
this point, however, we consider the issue of whether or not field-
based experiences are truly examples of clinical learning. The reform literature has typically used the terms *field-based* and *clinical*
as virtually interchangeable concepts, and there is a strong tendency to include *experiential learning* as a synonym for these terms
as well. Although there is certainly some overlap among these
clearly related terms, there are also some critical differences that
need to be understood if we are to discuss potential changes in
professional development opportunities for school administrators.

Griffin (1986) reviewed the literature on clinical approaches to
teacher education and identified seven critical features that need to
be present "whether the program is at the preservice, induction, or
inservice levels of implementation" (p. 7). In order for a program to
be truly a "clinical" experience, it must be embedded in a school
context and be (1) context-sensitive, (2) purposeful and articulated,
(3) participatory and collaborative, (4) knowledge-based, (5) ongoing, (6) developmental, and (7) analytic and reflective. Most current
suggestions for improving administrator professional development
suggest that clinical programs are experiences that are embedded
within a school context, but Griffin's conceptualization suggests
that there is considerably more to clinical education than merely
putting people out in schools for part of their training. All the
issues raised by Griffin suggest that there is a type of continuing
relationship fostered between the learner and those individuals,
either in local schools or at the university level, who will work
conscientiously with students to help make sense out of what is seen
in the field.

As we will indicate in a later chapter, we believe that there is
value in learning in field-based settings, whether the learners are
aspiring administrators or experienced administrators. However, it
is simplistic to think that merely putting people out into school
settings more frequently will automatically improve the quality of
educational leadership in this country. A more systematic and comprehensive form of change is needed to improve the professional
development of American school administrators, regardless of the
prevailing philosophical orientation to administration, and apart
from whether individuals are involved with preservice preparation,
induction, or inservice education. We propose, through the remain-

ing chapters of this book, a new conceptualization of administrator professional development.

A Tridimensional Model for Professional Development

There is sufficient cause to suggest that some new ways to prepare and support educational leaders in the United States, if not around the world, might be proposed. There is an uneasiness, even some open dissatisfaction, with what is taking place in schools generally, and that has been reflected in the plethora of recent reform proposals. An increasingly common view of the ways in which existing problems in schools may be solved involves the redefinition of traditional educational roles and responsibilities, and also the existing images of professionalism for educators. These insights regarding potential improvement for schools have also been acknowledged in the arena of professional development for school administrators, with the result being an increased focus on such things as the development of more effective collaborative relationships between universities and local education agencies, and the increase of clinical experiences as part of administrative development. Coupled with all of these potential reform practices is an increasing recognition that, first, many new principals will be entering the field during the next few years, and, second, that there is a data base that currently exists about the learning needs of administrators (both experienced and beginning). These factors might serve as the basis for the design of more effective professional development. Despite all of these observations, however, the general state of the art regarding how administrators are prepared and supported remains remarkably unchanged (Achilles, 1987; Daresh, 1988).

One might argue that, because excellent educational leaders continue to be found, and given that they have been prepared for their role through existing practices, a lot of what is now taking place "ain't broke," so there's no need to "fix" things. Any proposal for changing the preservice preparation, induction, and inservice education of school administrators must be sensitive to the likelihood that some of what is now taking place is good, but also that it could be better with some modification. The result is the development of what we describe as a *tridimensional conceptualization* for the professional development of school administrators, a model that includes academic preparation, field-based learning, and personal and professional formation. Lortie (1975) suggested that there are three sources of occupational socialization: (1) formal education, (2) apprenticeship, and (3) "learning by doing." In the chapters that follow, the argument will be advanced that people must receive preparation and support for their leadership roles through equal attention to strong academic preparation (Lortie's view of "formal education"); realistic guided practice in the field (the "apprenticeship" and "learning-by-doing" components of Lortie); and, perhaps most important, attention to the typically ignored issue of the formation of aspiring administrators who will need to cope personally and professionally with the ambiguities associated with the responsibilties of school leadership. The three component elements of the tridimensional conceptualization are shown in Figure 1.1

The tridimensional conceptualization is described as a way to address more directly some of the perceived shortcomings of many present efforts to prepare and support educational leaders. Our concern here is with three distinct phases that make up professional development: preservice preparation, induction, and inservice education. The tridimensional conceptualization has important implications for each of these three phases.

Preservice preparation consists of those learning activities and other processes that take place prior to initial job placement. Recruitment, selection, training, licensure, and placement into a first job are all components of the preservice preparation phase.

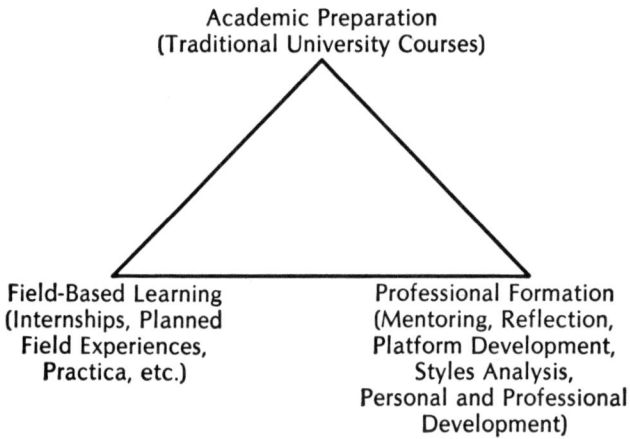

FIGURE 1.1 • *Diagram representing the tridimensional conceptualization of professional development for administrators.*

Induction may be defined as the period in a person's career when he or she is in a new position in an organization, under a new role definition. The process of induction is something that is not necessarily concluded after one year in a new job. Induction may take several years to complete, depending on conditions in the organization, the nature of the role, and the characteristics of the individual.

Inservice education consists of learning opportunities that are provided to individuals while they are actually engaged in a job. These opportunities may be directed specifically at helping a person to perform the duties of a particular job more efficiently or effectively, or they may be directed toward the personal growth and development of the person performing a job, regardless of the expectations of the job.

All of the elements of the tridimensional conceptualization may be included in all three phases of ongoing professional development. What differs, of course, may be the relative strengths of academic preparation, field-based learning, and personal and professional formation as a person moves from preservice preparation to induction to inservice education. The diagram shown in Figure 1.2 is an effort to depict the likely relative balance of the different dimensions in each of the phases.

When people first enter the field of educational administration (preservice preparation), they presumably have little basic information concerning the nature of school management. What is adminis-

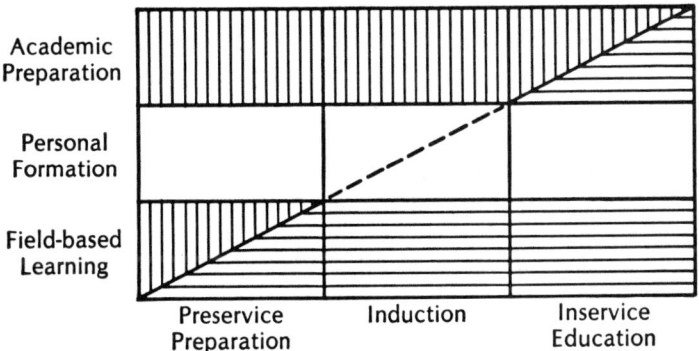

FIGURE 1.2 • *Diagram representing the elements of the tridimensional conceptualization of professional development and the three major phases of career development.*

tration? How does one define *plenary power?* What are the constitutional bases for the systems of public education that are found in the fifty states? These are examples of the kinds of issues that are fundamental to any appreciation of the concept of educational management in the United States. They are best learned through fairly straightforward strategies in classrooms, or through reading, or through other methods that comprise academic preparation. As Figure 1.2 suggests, the majority of one's learning in the earliest phases of preservice preparation might involve heavy emphasis, if not exclusive reliance, on academic preparation.

As people progress through the phases of their careers, learning will occur more frequently from an experiential base. As one learns a field more completely through academic preparation, experience in the field (i.e., field-based learning) will have more relevance. For example, after one has a fundamental idea of what "formative evaluation of teachers" might be, witnessing a clinical supervision conference will make more sense. While academic preparation decreases throughout a career and field-based learning increases, there is never a point where either of these dimensions disappears entirely. Even the newest beginner to preservice preparation can learn experientially, and the most experienced practitioners still should occasionally read a book or attend a lecture to learn about developments in their field.

The dimension that tends to remain constant throughout all phases of a person's career is personal and professional formation. The need to engage in reflection, to think about one's personal ethical stances and one's commitment to a profession, is constant, although the issues that might be considered will differ. A beginning administrator's lack of understanding of what it means to be "the boss" will not be relevant for a ten-year veteran of the principal's office. But moral dilemmas that require one to examine personal value systems can be found at all points in a person's professional life. Mentoring might be seen as a consistent activity from preservice to inservice. Again, the nature of collegial supportive relationships will change with experience, but more time on a job does not make a person more likely to profit from having an understanding and patient colleague.

We need to examine further the assumptions concerning the relative potencies of each of the dimensions at different career phases. Academic preparation, field-based learning, and personal and professional formation can be a part of every administrator's professional life. In the remaining chapters of this book, we look at the dimensions of the model in greater detail, and also at some of the major issues that are related to the three phases of professional development. After explaining more fully the features of academic preparation (Chapter 2), field-based learning (Chapter 3), and personal and professional formation (Chapter 4), we devote the next three sections of the book to a review of concerns and issues related to preservice preparation, induction, and inservice education.

Summary

Three forces that contribute to a comprehensive understanding of professional development for school administrators are described in this chapter. First, a framework was presented that explained the historical development of educational administration in terms of three alternative philosophical orientations: scientific management, human relations, and human resource development. For each of these approaches, the major assumptions were noted, along with implications for professional development. None of these views is "perfect," nor is any of the approaches completely wrong. Rather, it was suggested that anyone charged with the responsibility of addressing the professional development needs of administrators needs to be aware of the fact that the three orientations are alive and present in the literature and are reflected in the practices of many school leaders.

The second issue addressed in this chapter concerned the tridimensional conceptualization of administrator professional development. In this model, we suggest that three dimensions need to be included in any effective approach to preparing and supporting school administrators: academic preparation, field-based learning, and personal and professional formation. Some of the most important characteristics of each of these dimensions were noted.

The third issue that we addressed concerned the broad definition of professional development that we have selected to frame our discussion throughout this book. We speak of *professional development* not as a convenient substitute for terms like *inservice education* or *staff development*. Instead, when we use the term, we are describing three distinct phases of an individual's career: preservice preparation, induction, and ongoing inservice education. We believe that these three phases need to be understood in concert; they are interactive in nature, and an appreciation of preservice leads to discussions of induction concerns, which in turn are related to inservice education. Our goal in this book is to indicate that issues of professional development cannot be defined as isolated and separated events in a person's career. They must be viewed more holistically.

References

Achilles, Charles M. (1985). *Unlocking some mysteries of administration: A reflective perspective.* Unpublished briefing paper presented to the National Commission on Excellence in Educational Administration.

Culbertson, Jack A. (1988). A century's quest for a knowledge base. In Norman J. Boyan (Ed.), *Handbook of research on educational administration.* White Plains, NY: Longman.

Daresh, John C. (1988, April). *The preservice preparation of American educational administrators: Retrospect and prospect.* Invited paper presented at the meeting of the British Educational Management and Administration Society, Cardiff, Wales.

Dewey, John. (1938). *Education and experience.* New York: Macmillan.

Griffin, Gary A. (1986). Clinical teacher education. In James Hoffman & Sara Edwards (Eds.), *Reality and reform in clinical teacher education.* New York: Random House

Griffiths, Daniel, Stout, Robert, & Forsyth, Patrick. (1988). *Leaders for tomorrow's schools: The report of the National Commission.* Berkeley, CA: McCutchan.

Lortie, D. (1975). *Schoolteacher.* Chicago: University of Chicago Press.

Neale, Daniel C., Bailey, William J., & Ross, Billy E. (1981). *Strategies for school improvement: Cooperative planning and organization development.* Boston: Allyn and Bacon.

Taylor, Frederick W. (1916). *Principles of scientific management.* Bulletin of the Taylor Society.

Villers, Raymond. (1960). *Dynamic management in industry.* Englewood Cliffs, NJ: Prentice-Hall.

CHAPTER TWO

Academic Preparation

The first of three dimensions of our model for administrator professional development is *academic preparation*. By far, this has served as the primary approach that has been utilized to provide aspiring administrators with the knowledge base needed to carry out their jobs.

Traditional approaches to the preparation of educational administrators have emphasized the acquisition of the requisite knowledge related to the effective performance of administrative tasks and responsibilities through the medium of graduate-level university courses. Depending on certain local variables, such as the requirements of state departments of education across the nation, universities have offered the courses that have been needed by individuals who wanted to meet minimum licensing requirements. As a result, courses in such fields as school law, finance, curriculum development, personnel management and collective bargaining, and home–school–community relations are often viewed as critical aspects of the skills generally associated with more effective administrative performance. It is in this context that they are provided to those who seek administrative certificates. In general, there is a long-standing tradition in the United States suggesting that those who succeed in university courses are well prepared, and that they are ready to step immediately into administrative roles in schools (Burke, 1934). The view that administrative preparation would be best tied to the completion of academic goals is shown in the following statement by Paul Jacobson and William Reavis (1941):

> *For those who aspire to the most responsible positions [in educational administration], it will probably be necessary in the future to acquire training represented by the doctor's degree. Such*

*training is now possessed only be a very small percentage of
school principals. Those who have the training find their professional qualifications in great demand.*

Jacobson's and Reavis's observations about supply and demand
for administrators with doctoral degrees may no longer be accurate,
but the belief that there is some inherent value in the pursuit of
knowledge through university coursework as a part of preservice
training is alive and quite well. One of the recommendations of the
National Policy Board for the Preparation of Educational Administrators, issued in 1989, was that a minimal level of preparation for
the licensing of any school administrator should be the Ed.D. degree.

Assumptions and Rationale for Academic Preparation

The reliance on university courses as a way to prepare individuals
for roles in school administration is rooted deeply in a number of
rather clear assumptions. These are related to the value of conventional courses serving as a proper strategy to be followed in the
process of assisting in occupational or professional socialization.
Blumberg and Greenfield (1980) defined this as something "by
which a person learns and performs according to the norms, values,
and behaviors held to be necessary for performing a particular role"
(p. 221). Daniel Duke (1987), in his analysis of the ways in which
educational administrators learn how to provide instructional
leadership in their schools, noted that formal academic preparation
is the way normally used to carry out the professional socialization
process by exposing future administrators to their adopted area of
specialization through "course content, [and] contact with professors, practitioners, and peers" (p. 267).

Academic preparation in the form of university-based management coursework has been assumed to be an effective and efficient
way to help future administrators develop strong conceptual appreciation and understanding of a complex and ambiguous field of
professional practice. University courses have the potential to provide information that may be used by the future or present administrator to address many complex conceptual issues and problems, for
which there may not be many clear, practical, how-to-do-it solutions. Further, academic preparation through university courses

may be viewed as a way to enable people to comprehend basic facts, terms, and issues that serve as supplements to the larger field of administration. Examples include the areas of law, finance, personnel management, and facilities planning. Courses are useful ways of helping people acquire some of the basic "language" and knowledge base of their newly chosen field of practice. It is simpler, for example, to learn the basic characteristics associated with procedural due process through a lecture in a school law course than it might be to obtain this same information through some other learning source.

The theoretical assumptions that serve as the basis for the academic preparation dimension generally come from a view that holds that learning is essentially the product of a process referred to as "information assimilation" (Little, 1983). Here, the primary medium of learning is symbolic, where words or numbers are used as a way to describe and provide meanings to complex features of reality. Instructional techniques associated with this model normally include lectures and, at times, seminar discussions that are led by an individual viewed as an expert in the content to be presented. Learning tends to be viewed as an activity that takes place in lecture halls, classrooms, and libraries. The information assimilation model of learning and teaching may be depicted in the steps of the cyclical model shown in Figure 2.1.

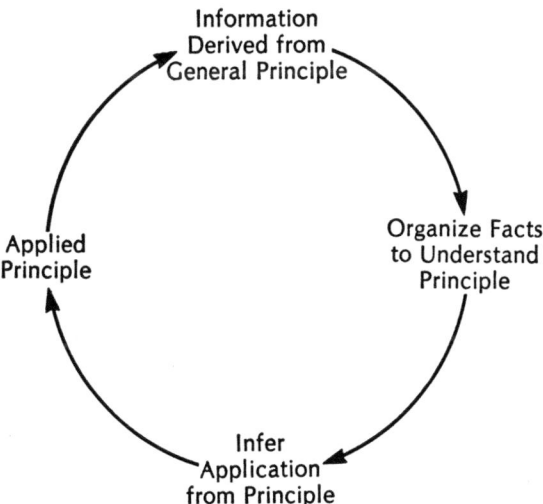

FIGURE 2.1 • *Information assimilation model of learning.*

Little (1983, p. 9) described the sequential steps of the information assimilation process in the following way:

> *As a first step, symbolic information is provided about what is considered in general principle. The next step is to process bits of information (facts) so that the general principle is understood. For example, if the great principle is that solids, liquids, and gases are the forms of matter with the operational condition being the relative concentration of molecules, understanding is enhanced by the information that ice, water, and steam are all forms of the same compound. The third step is to infer the distance between the molecules and thus transform water into steam. The final component is to apply the principle correctly—to see whether what is supposed to happen actually happens.*

The traditional guardians of the academic preparation dimension have been faculties in educational administration. This makes sense because the model of information assimilation has a need for some identified group to focus its attention on the business of knowledge production (to start the cycle), rather than engage solely in knowledge utilization. The best people to do this tend to be professors. Those who live in the "ivory tower" are normally able (and are usually encouraged) to engage in the type of systematic inquiry that must take place in an environment not necessarily burdened by the "noise" and daily crises found in most schools. Some group, such as the university faculty, must have the time to look at the broader issues that go beyond the solution of problems in the here and now, and often the best way for these perpectives to be shared with the practitioner community is through the familiar mechanism known as the university course.

Limitations on Academic Preparation

Academic preparation, particularly when it is defined primarily in terms of university coursework, is far from what may be considered a comprehensive approach to the ways in which future administrators are made ready for their first jobs. It is not possible to obscure totally some of the shortcomings of this practice. Perhaps the most fundamental problem is that, in most cases, the content of university courses related to educational management is based almost exclusively on selections and choices made by university faculty who often act as self-defined experts in the teaching fields of their choice. The self-interests of the academic, campus-based community, therefore, not only are primarily served, but often are the *only* priorities and interests that are addressed. Expertise, in the context of the university world, is defined largely in terms of a professor's knowledge base and decision-making processes alone, acquired usually through personal engagement in ongoing research, or through the combining and synthesis of the research findings of others. There is frequently little demonstration of a concern for practical expertise and the real-world application of research-based knowledge. A well-known professor, for example, might know much about research on personnel management but have no skill at actually working in a positive or productive way with his or her colleagues—something that would probably bar him or her from a job related to personnel work in the "real world" of most school systems. Rarely are clients (past, present, or future) ever consulted regarding the nature of what is to be taught through the medium of university courses. We make no attempt here to suggest that professors should somehow be bound to make their curricular choices based only on some sort of consensus decision-making process. Rather, we believe that dialogue between practitioners and academicians might be encouraged in the hope that it will yield some important insights into the ideal content to be included as part of academic preparation.

Another traditional drawback to university-based academic preparation concerns the issue of "how" the content of most courses is presented for student learning. As noted earlier, the university course makes almost exclusive use of the information assimilation model of learning. As a result, there is great reliance on the lecture, with its almost complete emphasis on one-way communication patterns from a professor to the students as passive learners. If this large-group technique, which normally causes students to be highly reactive learners, is ever modified, it is still likely to involve the forms of instruction that are largely classroom-bound. Rarely do university faculty incorporate learning activities that would enable students of administration actually to go out and "taste" the reality of leadership in school settings. To be sure, some professors make serious efforts to expand their instructional repertoire by requiring students to interview practicing administrators out in the field, observe school board and other meetings, and conduct community surveys, or by inviting local school practitioners to appear in their classes as guest speakers in a sort of show-and-tell arrangement. These are all commendable efforts to make traditional classes more relevant and lively, but they are of lasting value only if they are tied in some thoughtful way to the instructional objectives of classes, and if sufficient follow-up analysis and dialogue are also provided. If they are viewed primarily as extra projects, assigned to students out of a vague notion that they might be "good experiences," they may be much more valuable as ornamentation than they are as vital parts of student learning about the practice of effective educational administration.

Other shortcomings of academic preparation of school leaders that is based primarily or solely on university coursework are identified in a considerable amount of recent criticism of this form of learning that has been included in much of the literature related to the reform of preservice preparation practices. Edwin Bridges (1982), for example, described typical leadership training programs that are university-bound as failing to socialize people to the realities of leadership because, among other things, they tend to emphasize the acquisition of written skills despite the fact that leaders must learn to function in a highly oral world. Present courses prepare prospective leaders to be "thinkers" rather than "doers." This is not an entirely unappealing scenario, of course, as one hopes that school administrators will be people who demonstrate well-developed thinking skills. We would hardly advocate a system where administrators are simply trained to do their jobs as mere technicians of educational management.

Charles Achilles (1987), a frequent critic of the ways in which people are prepared to serve as school administrators, has noted some other severe limitations on most existing university-directed preparation programs because such efforts rely on courses that are not:

1. . . . taken in any particularly thoughtful sequence;
2. . . . differentiated according to levels of administration (principalship or superintendency), or to varying degree levels (M.A., Specialist, or Ph.D/Ed.D.);
3. . . . designed with some type of apparent conceptual framework
4. . . . developed with an underlying reliance on learning theory (or, in fact, any visible overarching theory base). This is particularly true with regard to any acknowledged reliance on adult learning theory.

5. . . . closely aligned with desired outcomes, or coordinated with the work that administrators do . . . or should do;
6. . . . typically related to rigorous evaluation, either singly or for their contribution to the development of a vision driving a total administrator preparation program.

No doubt other objections and limitations might also be voiced regarding the quality of courses that are used in many existing administrator preparation programs. But there are values to be found in these traditional forms of learning as well.

Promising Practices

The picture we have painted in this chapter may have suggested that all university-based academic preparation programs for educational administrators are without merit. That would be a most unfortunate depiction of what is going on across the nation. Many universities are engaged in the development of new approaches to the preparation of school leaders that emphasize very creative efforts to improve the quality of academic programs. Three such efforts that are highlighted here include frameworks used to guide the academic preparation programs at the University of Northern Colorado, the State University of New York at Buffalo, and The Ohio State University.

University of Northern Colorado

The University of Northern Colorado has recently been involved in a major effort to transform its traditional approach to administrative preparation from a reliance on completion of a series of required courses to a more holistic approach. A goal of the faculty has been to shift the preservice preparation of school leaders from a reliance on simply "collecting individual courses" in such traditional areas as school law, supervision, finance, school–community relations, and personnel to a set of integrated learning experiences that give students the needed knowledge, skills, and attitudes through a series of team-taught courses emphasizing more than the acquisition of pieces of knowledge that are attached to traditional courses.

The faculty began their developmental effort by deciding what ideas and values should be included as part of any learning experiences or courses that would make up their new vision of leadership development. The following seven statements were identified as central value statements or themes that would permeate all other activities of the leadership development program:

1. Learning, teaching, and collegiality are fundamental activities of educational organizations.
2. Moral and ethical imperatives drive leadership behavior.
3. Organizations are artifacts of a larger society.
4. Human growth and development are lifelong pursuits.
5. Validated knowledge and active inquiry form the basis of practice.
6. Leadership encompasses a learned set of knowledge, skills, and attitudes.
7. Leaders effect positive change in individuals and organizations.

These statements have been adopted as "nonnegotiable" values by the program faculty, to the extent that all other courses and activities are expected in some tangible way to reflect these concepts. The next step for the faculty has been the development of a set of core learning experiences which, in total, lead students to a clear conceptualization of leadership and its component responsibilities in school settings. It has also been necessary to make certain that these learning experiences, or courses, address the stated requirements of the state agency responsible for certifying school administrators, the Colorado Department of Education. The result has been the creation of a core set of five integrated learning experiences: "Understanding Self," "Shaping Organizations," "Understanding People," "Understanding Environments," and "Using Inquiry." A basic assumption in each of these learning experiences is that they are meant to serve the needs of individuals whose primary concern is preparation for an initial leadership role in schools. A brief description of the content in each of the five core experiences, depicted in relation to other courses required in the leadership preparation program in Figure 2.1, follows:

1. *Understanding Self: Developing a Personal Vision for Educational Leadership:* The primary objective of this course is to enable students to develop an appreciation of their fundamental values and attitudes toward school governance, administration, and

leadership. Considerable emphasis is placed on activities that will lead participants to appreciate their own strengths and weaknesses, particularly as these characteristics may suggest that they will achieve success and personal fulfillment in the role of educational leaders.

2. *Shaping Organizations: Management and Leadership in Education:* This course features learning experiences designed to help students develop an understanding of the basic structural components of educational organizations, along with the assumptions inherent in theoretical frameworks that describe organizational behavior. The relationship between the school and other organizations in society is also explored.

3. *Understanding People: Professional Development and Educational Leadership:* This course provides an overview of fundamental issues related to the development of personnel in educational organizations. Attention is directed toward entry-level knowledge of issues such as staff appraisal and adult learning and development.

4. *Understanding Environments: Social, Political, Economic, and Legal Influences:* This course provides basic information on concepts and practices related to both the internal and external environments of educational organizations. Information is provided concerning entry-level issues in the areas of school law, finance, and policy formation as characteristics of external environments. The development of curriculum and related policy in instructional improvement are considered as part of the analysis of the internal environment of the educational organization.

5. *Using Inquiry: Framing Problems and Making Decisions in Educational Leadership:* In this course, the primary goal is to help students develop an appreciation of alternative ways of knowing that are frequently used by school leaders, and how these alternative perspectives relate to leadership behavior in organizations.

As the model presented in Figure 2.2 shows, students at the University of Northern Colorado are also expected to participate in a number of other courses beyond the core learning experiences. Each student must select a seminar related to leadership at an appropriate role level in the organization. Each person must also participate in a seminar related to issues associated with the level of schooling in which the student will serve as a leader. Also, students must select from a variety of more traditional administrative courses in such areas as school law, finance, supervision, and so

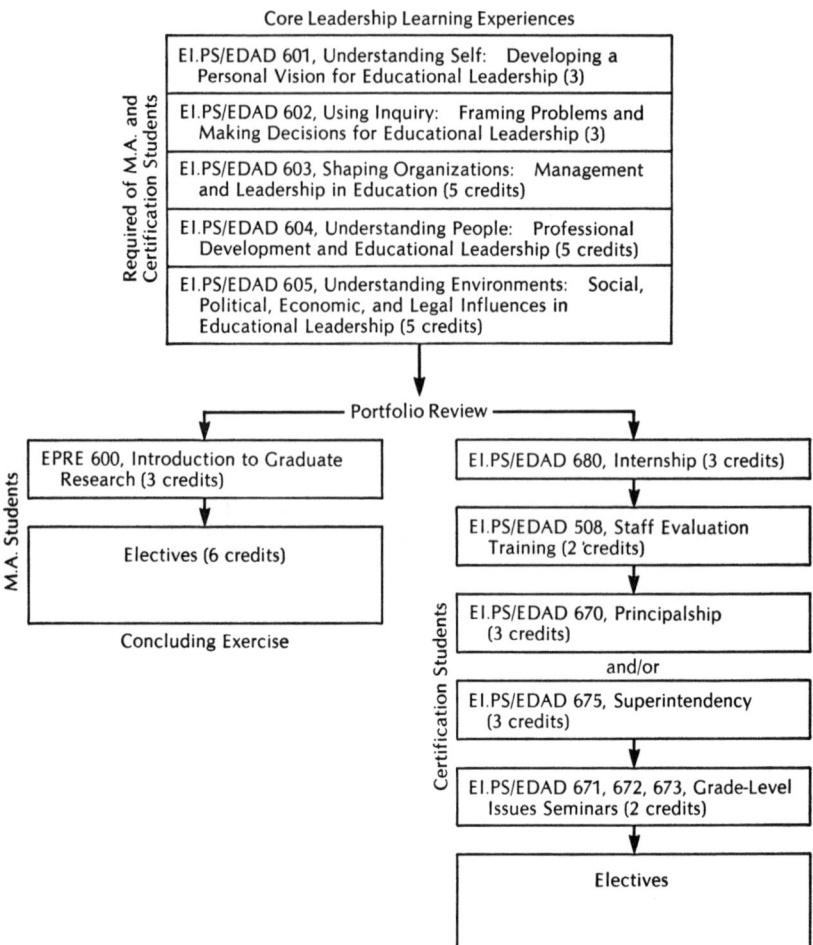

Core Leadership Learning Experiences

Required of M.A. and Certification Students

EI.PS/EDAD 601, Understanding Self: Developing a Personal Vision for Educational Leadership (3)

EI.PS/EDAD 602, Using Inquiry: Framing Problems and Making Decisions for Educational Leadership (3)

EI.PS/EDAD 603, Shaping Organizations: Management and Leadership in Education (5 credits)

EI.PS/EDAD 604, Understanding People: Professional Development and Educational Leadership (5 credits)

EI.PS/EDAD 605, Understanding Environments: Social, Political, Economic, and Legal Influences in Educational Leadership (5 credits)

Portfolio Review

M.A. Students

EPRE 600, Introduction to Graduate Research (3 credits)

Electives (6 credits)

Concluding Exercise

Certification Students

EI.PS/EDAD 680, Internship (3 credits)

EI.PS/EDAD 508, Staff Evaluation Training (2 credits)

EI.PS/EDAD 670, Principalship (3 credits)

and/or

EI.PS/EDAD 675, Superintendency (3 credits)

EI.PS/EDAD 671, 672, 673, Grade-Level Issues Seminars (2 credits)

Electives

FIGURE 2.2 • *General model illustrating courses and other learning experiences required for the initial leadership preparation program at the University of Northern Colorado, Greeley.*

forth to identify at least four elective courses that will help them learn in depth about an area of educational leadership that has particular relevance to their professional goals. Finally, each student must complete a supervised internship, in accordance with state department expectations for initial certification.

The University of Northern Colorado program has been designed to address a number of recent criticisms. A common concern has been that leadership programs have traditionally treated all students as if they were the same. For example, there has been an implicit assumption that all students in a course on school law had the same backgrounds or interests. More often than not, beginning teachers are seated in law courses next to individuals with many years of administrative experience, who are required to take the same course but with considerably different objectives. The Northern Colorado program is also directed toward an attempt to provide some instructional sequence. For example, the "Understanding Self" course is meant to be the first course taken by any student pursuing the leadership development program because it is designed with activities that will help students decide if they are truly interested in following a path toward a formal leadership role in schools.

State University of New York at Buffalo

The faculty of educational administration in the Department of Educational Organization, Administration, and Policy (EOAP) at the State University of New York at Buffalo engaged in a planning process during the early 1980s to devise a more effective approach to preparing individuals to assume leadership roles in educational organizations (State University of New York, 1981). This work was based on the view that the central mission of the educational administration should be:

To produce graduates who possess intellectual and performance skills that result in superior accomplishment in leadership roles in educational administration.

In its efforts to build strategies that could increase the likelihood that this mission could be achieved, the faculty turned its attention to the development of a delivery system that could be followed by students. The fundamental assumption inherent in that system is that leadership includes:

The capacity to comprehend future states of affairs (objective context) that are better for all people (human context), and the ability to devise patterns of means or strategies that lead to those desirable states of affairs in educational systems (action domain).

This view of the requisite skills associated with effective administrative performance has been translated into action through the implementation of a conceptual framework used to unify existing university coursework. Each student of educational administration is expected to pursue coursework in three major areas: Component I (Common Learnings), Component II (Concentrations), and Component III (Individual Development). Each of these component areas includes coursework and other learning experiences that have been designed to be consistent with the overall mission of the program area.

Component I: Common Learnings

Here, the student is expected to build basic performance competency in a number of common learning areas:

1. *Systematic Inquiry in Educational Administration:* This involves an awareness of problem-solving processes, theory and research, and skills in the specification of problems and interpretation of analyzed data. This area is introduced early in a student's program.
2. *Communication:* This area emphasizes skills of interpersonal communication and associated techniques for understanding formal and informal aspects of these.
3. *Value Analysis:* Values are involved in all administrative decisions. An awareness of values and their formation, coupled with skills in analyzing the value of positions of personnel, forms the fundamental competency expectations in this area.
4. *Human Relations:* Associated with communication and value analysis, the basics of this area involve an awareness of cultural differences and similarities and the skills of operating with genuine interest in others as valuable individuals.
5. *Organization Analysis:* Because graduates of the educational administration program will be working in or with organizations, it is essential that they understand organizational components and have skills in structuring and redesigning organizations for goal attainment.
6. *Planning:* There is an increasing awareness of the importance of planning in and for education. Knowledge and application of selected planning models are essential as a foundation for this competency.
7. *Evaluation:* To plan, create, or build without ascertaining the effects of such actions is potentially hazardous. An educational leader needs to understand the concept of evaluation and be able to apply appropriate techniques in day-to-day operations.

8. *Change:* Fundamental to the concept of leadership is the ability to move an organization toward desired ends. This requires an understanding of concepts of change and associated techniques of change agents.
9. *Decision Making:* A systematic approach to decision making is at the heart of educational administration.
10. *Educational Policy Formation:* This area relates to the understanding of the concepts of *policy, justice,* and *due process* in the educational sphere, and emphasizes approaches for developing, implementing, and changing these.
11. *Environments:* The learning-schooling environments are a concern for all school leaders. Awareness of the interactions between the internal environment (school building, classrooms) and external environment (community or social milieu), coupled with skills for controlling such interactions, is the focus of this area.
12. *Allocation of Resources:* The determination and distribution of human and material resources for effective educational outcomes require an understanding of certain resource models and the ability to apply them. These skills are sine qua non for educational leaders.
13. *Operations Research:* Quantitative techniques for modeling and decision making are increasing in number. Awareness of this area and skills relevant to the request for the specialization contribute to the uniqueness of program graduates.
14. *Observation:* Observing and describing are fundamental processes in all sciences. There are a multitude of approaches that may be more or less relevant to one concentration or another.

Component II: Concentrations

Students select one of four different areas of administration to serve as a concentration:

Educational Administration Policy This includes courses and seminars intended for students who wish to develop special competence in policy formulation, enactment, implementation, and evaluation in educational institutions.

The Educational Organization The focus here is on learning activities that stress the development of two leadership processes—diagnosis and intervention, and the implementation of these processes in educational organizations.

Planning and Operations Analysis This concentration focuses on understanding and skills related to improving educational organizations' effectiveness and efficiency. This is accomplished through analysis of existing systems and through design, implementation, and maintenance of optimal systems using methods normally classified under economic analysis, operations research, and systems analysis.

Instructional Systems: Design and Management This concentration focuses on the design of formal instructional systems for the efficient development of knowledge bases, skills, understandings, and attitudes among targeted clients. To prepare persons for design and management of specific educational delivery systems, students in this concentration must develop broad understandings of a number of contributing disciplines, including communication theory, sociology of knowledge, information theory, systems theory, and learning theory.

Component III: The Individual Component
Here, the educational administration program becomes highly individualized so that students are able to concentrate on original contributions to knowledge about organizations, administration of educational institutions, or policy development or implementation. This component focuses directly on the ability of the future leader to engage in systematic and original forms of inquiry related to topics in the field of educational administration.

The administrative preparation program at Buffalo has been devised as a way to provide students with a sequential approach to the acquisition of knowledge, attitudes, values, and skills associated with more effective performance.

The Ohio State University

The educational administration program at The Ohio State University, revised to meet new requirements of the Ohio Department of Education in 1985, is based on the assumption that school leaders are made ready to assume their future roles by following a structured instructional program. This instructional program, in turn, is built upon a set of nine themes selected by the program faculty as representative of critical issues faced by school leaders.

Theme 1: Learning

If the school's mission is to give students optimum opportunities to learn, then this mission must be the primary influence on administrative practice and must have significant implications for administrator training. The facilitation of learning is closely related to curriculum and instruction.

Theme 2: Equity

In the larger societal context, progress toward equity that was achieved in the 1960s and 1970s has slowed recently. However, the problem remains a continuing challenge for administrators. It is visible in inequitable financing arrangements; in sex, race, class, and other expressions of discrimination among students, staff, and parents; and in unequal learning opportunities within and between school systems. It is less visible, but always present, in routine practices at every level of educational organization. Equity, defined as fairness, is at the center of all student and staff personnel policies. Conditions affecting equity, then, pose deep and pervasive challenges to educational leaders.

Theme 3: The Individual in Society

The literature on administration and leadership is oriented to the collective aspects of organizations. In that view, organizations, not individuals, tend to think, choose, act, and respond to their environments. Yet the energy and potential for organizational productivity resides ultimately with individuals, as do capacities for critique, for initiative, for creativity, for progress, and even for survival. Without individuals, organizations are abstractions.

Those responsible for designing preparatory programs for educational administrators need to understand the "collective" bias of the literature on communities, institutions, organizations, groups, and the critical role individuals play in organizations.

Theme 4: Knowledge

Knowledge is an administrative tool that is significant in both the training and the performance of principals, superintendents, and other school personnel. It is also an important tool for professors of educational administration.

Theme 5: Curriculum

There is concern that programs have concentrated too much on organization and administration and not enough on curriculum—

a condition encouraged by separate and specialized academic units.

Theme 6: Instruction

If curriculum is defined as the *what* of the teaching process, then instruction may be viewed as the *how* of that process. Instruction is enhanced substantially by high-quality, readily available, and effectively used resources. Administrative support for the instructional process enhances both the quality and quantity of instruction.

Theme 7: Administration

Administration is concerned with effective and efficient organizational performance within a framework of established policy. School leaders are at the center of organizational communication networks. They also have the major responsibility for seeing that schools and school systems perform effectively and efficiently.

Theme 8: Politics

Educational administrators today continually work within the political arena as they discharge their responsibilities.

Theme 9: Leadership

Leadership plays a vital role in education. Societal events reinforce the importance of that role.

The University of Northern Colorado, the State University of New York at Buffalo, and The Ohio State University all offer important departures from many traditional university-based academic preparation programs in educational administration. There is no appreciable difference between the delivery strategies that are used at the three institutions; professors by and large continue to present information in lectures or through seminars and discussions. All three programs, however, have attempted to provide a type of broad conceptual framework that serves to organize individual required courses according to a broader set of goals and objectives. As a result, considerable improvement has been made beyond more conventional programs.

Summary

One of the three components of the tridimensional model of professional development for school administrators is academic preparation. In this chapter, this dimension was defined and described as learning about the work of administration through traditional university coursework. Although it was noted that some courses include required activities that take students outside of the classroom, the central ingredient in this component of professional development consists of learning in university classrooms through the application of an information assimilation model of learning.

The chapter included a review of the major assumptions that underlie the traditional reliance on academic preparation of school administrators. Included were several of the strengths and weaknesses of this approach to the ways in which educational leaders are made ready for their first jobs. Finally, information was provided about the educational leadership programs at three universities, all of which represent efforts to improve the quality of traditional academic preparation programs for educational administrators.

References

Achilles, Charles. (1987). *Unlocking some mysteries of administration: A reflective perspective.* Unpublished briefing paper submitted to the National Commission on Excellence in Educational Administration.

Blumberg, Arthur, & Greenfield, William. (1980). *The effective principal.* Boston: Allyn and Bacon.

Bridges, Edwin M. (1982). Research on the school administrator: State of the art. *Educational Administration Quarterly, 18,* 3:12–33.

Burke, A. J. (1934, October). Professional courses for school principals. *Educational Administration and Supervision, 20:* 506–512.

Duke, Daniel L. (1987). *School leadership and instructional improvement.* New York: Random House.

Jacobson, Paul B., & Reavis, William C. (1941). *Duties of school principals.* New York: Prentice-Hall.

Little, Thomas C. (1983). *History and rationale for experiential learning.* Resource Paper No. 20. Raleigh, NC: National Society for Internships and Experiential Learning.

National Policy Board on Administrative Preparation. (1989). *Executive Summary of the Report of the Policy Board.* Charlottesville, VA: The Board.

Ohio State University, The. (1985). *Proposed programs of administrative certification to the Ohio Department of Education.* Columbus: Department of Educational Policy and Leadership, College of Education.

State University of New York. (1981). *Educational administration programs.* Buffalo: College of Education, State University of New York at Buffalo.

CHAPTER THREE

Field-Based Learning

The second dimension of a comprehensive approach to professional development for school administrators consists of field-based learning, or "learning by doing" out in the real world of schools. In this chapter, we review some of the major characteristics of efforts to incorporate this mode of learning into preservice, induction, and inservice programs. We begin by looking at a number of fundamental assumptions normally associated with field-based learning. Next, we take a look at some of the strongest limitations to this approach. Finally, we present a number of promising practices in this area, including the use of full-time internships, part-time planned field experiences, and course-embedded learning opportunities for aspiring and practicing school administrators.

Assumptions of Field-Based Learning

The current view of many of the reformers of preparation and inservice education programs for school administrators seems to be that the improvement of training depends largely on the use of more field-based and experiential learning programs for aspiring and practicing administrators. From various sources, including the National Commission on Excellence in Educational Administration (Griffiths, Stout, & Forsyth, 1988), Goodlad (1984), Cornett (1983), Achilles (1987), and Baltzell and Dentler (1983), comes a clear and consistent call for administrative preparation programs to stop teaching about administration and, instead, direct much greater attention toward helping people learn how to administer schools. The suggestions in most proposals call for practical, hands-on learning to be incorporated into the curricula of preparation programs. A suggestion by the Southern Regional Education Board (SREB) in 1983 (Cornett) is representative of many other recent statements:

Colleges need to develop programs solidly grounded in theory, but which also include some practicality. Internships, offered in full cooperation with local school districts, are one solution.

At present there is a strong tendency to move toward preservice preparation programs that are largely field-based in nature. A recent proposal by James LaPlant (1988) took this idea even further by suggesting that universities should probably get out of the administrator preparation business entirely and turn it over to practitioners in the field. According to this view, universities would become places where people are educated through academic preparation alone, as described in the previous chapter, not "trained" in ways that practitioners are much better able to do. These suggestions may raise the logical question, "If practitioners are really better prepared to train people, then why don't we always see better practice in the field after people have concluded their university coursework?" Such discussions may have the unintended consequence of further distancing university faculty members from being able to work productively with their colleagues in the field.

The literature provides a fairly well defined picture of what "field-based" programs are. Daresh and LaPlant (1985) reviewed descriptions of the characteristics of programs in institutions affiliated with the University Council for Educational Administration (UCEA) and discovered:

1. Typical field-based programs are not required of all students enrolled in educational administration graduate programs, but, rather, only of students seeking an administrative credential. When required, field-based activities most often occur near the end of the student's program.

2. Most programs operate in basically the same fashion: Students are expected to register for an academic credit-bearing course entitled "Administrative Internship," "Planned Field Experience," or some other similar title. They spend anywhere from 10 to 40 hours during a term observing a practitioner who, in turn, assigns the student some tasks or projects to be carried out under his or her supervision.

3. Field-based programs normally provide academic credit, but student evaluation is of the pass/fail variety. Responsibility for evaluating student performance most often resides with the university faculty member who coordinates the practicum.

4. The university faculty coordinator is usually the only faculty member in the department who works with students enrolled in

the practicum. Other than initial academic advising processes for students, the majority of the academic program faculty are not actively involved in supervising practica. In fact, in many institutions, the person responsible for supervising internships and planned field experiences is not a regular university faculty member but, rather, a limited-term adjunct clinical instructor or lecturer.

5. The duration of most field experiences is dictated by the length of the university's term, not by the time required to complete a project.

6. Students who participate in most internships or field experiences are not paid for their work. As a result, the majority of participants in field-based administrator preparation programs today are involved on a part-time basis while attempting to continue with teaching or other professional responsibilities in the same schools where they are also engaged in their practica.

Field-based programs may serve as ways for aspiring administrators to apply theoretical learning and develop their managerial and leadership skills and competencies. Field-based programs, when well designed and in their ideal states, may be used to help people gain important insights into the ways in which schools are actually administered, acquire and develop some practical skills through participation in a wide range of daily administrative duties, and apply knowledge learned in the university to a real-life setting. Field-based programs allow students of administration to witness the practical aspects of running schools, particularly if they are able to work with talented administrators as effective role models.

Limitations on Field-Based Learning

Despite the persistent emphasis on the need for field-based learning programs to serve as a foundation in strategies used to prepare school administrators, there may be some severe shortcomings to this approach. These limitations are most pronounced when field activities are not combined with other dimensions of preservice learning, particularly strong academic preparation. In the field of teacher education, many authorities have questioned some of the assumptions traditionally tied to the practicum as a learning device. Beginning with John Dewey (1938) and continuing with the more contemporary observations of David Berliner (1984), Donald

Cruickshank and William Armaline (1986), and Kenneth Zeichner (1985), numerous cautions have been raised to suggest that field-based learning experiences may often be viewed as miseducative, and that they frequently serve to create cognitive and behavioral traps that are apt to close avenues to conceptual and social change that may be well warranted (Daresh & Pape, 1987). In short, field-based learning programs often serve to prepare people only for what the world is like at present and for what things were like in the past. Little is done to help them anticipate what reality might be like in the future. The field experience for preparing educational leaders cannot be viewed in the same vein as the apprenticeship used in the training of plumbers and electricians, who are typically prepared for their work in the future by learning many time-honored techniques that have appeared to work well in the past.

In his analysis of the nature of the work carried out by school principals, Kent Peterson (1985) concluded that there are a number of restrictions to the use of field-based learning experiences:

> *The principal's work . . . is complex and comprised of a wide range of demands and expectations. The content of learning of necessity should cover most of the complexity. . . . Principals, like other managers, must develop the necessary skills and knowledge . . . in order to run an effective school. Some of these can only be learned on the job while others are best learned in a combination of formal training and on-the-job learning.*

We do not suggest that field-based learning experiences should be excluded from preservice administrator preparation programs. To the contrary, our view is that they may be extremely powerful ways for people to learn about their craft. On the other hand, because of some of the limitations noted here, too great a reliance on the practicum would be as unwise as attempts to prepare people for leadership roles "by the book"—only through academic preparation in traditional university coursework.

Promising Practices

Although the most recent calls for reform in educational adminis-tration training programs have suggested that more field-based learning opportunities are needed, such calls are hardly new. For many years, there has been a belief that, because school administration is truly an applied field of learning, "good" programs would necessarily include some ways for students to engage in hands-on learning. As a result, numerous efforts exist to incorporate field-based learning into administrator preparation programs. We review three generic models of such efforts that have been widely used over the years. These include full-time administrative internships, part-time planned field experiences, and course-embedded programs offering students the chance to learn by doing.

Full-Time Internships

For several years, the approach to field-based learning that has often been described as most desirable in terms of helping aspiring administrators learn more about their craft has been the full-time paid internship. In this model, the aspiring administrator, normally a full-time teacher in search of a career change, is given a leave from the classroom for either a semester or an entire school year. During that time, the individual is placed into a school or system on a full-time basis to serve as an administrative assistant to a veteran principal or central office administrator. A variation on this model might have the aspiring leader serving as a special intern who works with many administrators in a school district. Ideally, the intern would be released from all teaching responsibilities to live the life of a school administrator as completely as possible. The aspiring administrator would be expected to adhere to all typical job requirements expected of veteran administrators, including conformity with regular work hours, attendance at meetings, and supervision of weekend and evening school-sponsored activities. In short, an administrative internship of this type is analogous to a total-immersion foreign language program, where an individual becomes involved with a new language and culture—a whole new way of life—as quickly as possible. In return for this investment of time and energy, the intern administrator is paid a stipend by the school system in which he or she serves. Often the stipend is equivalent to the salary that the intern would earn if he or she were a teacher in the district.

This approach has numerous advantages. The intern is exposed to a full range of responsibilities that might be faced by any practicing administrator. These include both positive and frustrating experiences. The full-time internship gives the learner a fairly clear picture of what professional life will be like on a sustained basis. Like the internship in medical education, this approach to learning about educational administration gives people a chance to acquire and practice technical skills while under the care and direct supervision of an experienced practitioner. The intern also benefits from this program because he or she is able to gain work experience long before taking a first job. Participation in a full-time administrative internship is a way for a person to acquire a significant advantage over other competitors for beginning administrative positions.

From the perspective of the sponsoring school systems, interns have great value as inexpensive administrative assistants who relieve some of the burdens of full-time principals and others. Such a benefit is currently being realized by many school districts in Utah which, because of a statewide moratorium imposed on the construction of new school buildings, face the problem of large enrollments in many elementary schools, with enrollments in excess of 1,000 pupils not uncommon. Brigham Young University has developed an innovative approach to administrator training known as the Leadership Preparation Program (LPP) which requires that participants spend part of one school year as full-time interns. In return for making this powerful learning opportunity available to student interns, local school districts get much-needed relief in the form of additional administrative personnel who work in buildings to reduce the load for principals.

There are also some drawbacks to full-time internships. Perhaps the most serious is the fact that such programs are extremely costly to operate. What the addition of an intern to a district really means is that the cost of an additional full-time teacher must be added to a system's payroll. Such a commitment may be rare, as each penny is usually held up to considerable public scrutiny. The addition of staff who are being paid to learn about and help administrators—whom the public traditionally views as overpaid and underworked nonnecessities—may be politically unwise. Further, in many smaller districts across the country there is simply no money available for such a program. In short, despite the great benefits to learners and districts alike, numerous studies of administrative internships over the years have shown that such efforts cost more than many school systems are willing to pay.

Another persistent concern about internship programs is that they may do little more than perpetuate undesirable existing practices. It is a frequent criticism of internships that many of these arrangements simply offer newcomers to administration the opportunity to follow and repeat the approaches demonstrated by more experienced principals or superintendents. The concern here is that administrative solutions from the past are often not appropriate for the problems of the future. Later, we discuss the characteristics of effective mentoring programs for aspiring and practicing administrators. We believe that the adoption of such programs may be an effective strategy to follow in making certain that intern programs do not become "cloning" efforts.

Despite the limitations mentioned here in the use of internships, this model of field-based learning continues to be introduced as a highly desirable one. During the late 1940s and early 1950s, for example, Clarence Newell was an advocate of the use of full-time internships for future administrators. His efforts led to the creation of one of the first such programs at the University of Maryland in 1951 (Newell, 1952).

The pressure to increase the number of internships available for aspiring administrators during the 1950s was relatively short lived. Evaluations of programs provided two consistent findings. First, programs were viewed as effective and highly desirable components of administrative preservice preparation. Second, they were far too costly for most school systems to support on a continuing basis. As a result, efforts to increase the number of active full-time internships that were available across the nation were curtailed until the next great push in this area came about during the late 1960s and early 1970s. A large part of the National Association of Secondary School Principals' (NASSP) Model Schools Project involved the use of intern experiences designed to train individuals to assume the role of principal in highly innovative high schools across the nation (Trump, 1971). The other major effort made to encourage the use of full-time internships came about with the support of the Ford Foundation for the efforts of five universities in New York State during the 1960s to develop active intern programs (Holloway & Morgan, 1967). Again, both of these programs were well received for the time in which they were receiving substantial amounts of financial support.

Full-time administrative internships have remained central to many discussions concerning the reform of preservice programs over the past few years. There have been local efforts to encourage work in this area, but the same problems that brought about the demise of most earlier internships have continued to plague these programs. There is great verbal support but little accompanying financial commitment. When local school systems must face difficult choices regarding the investment of limited financial resources, leadership development activities are usually left off the priority list. The internship is one of these activities that could be quite effective, but costly.

Planned Field Experiences

Designers of preparation programs for administrators have come to understand a number of things over the years. First, it is desirable to find opportunities for aspiring leaders to learn by doing. Second, most future administrators come from the ranks of present-day classroom teachers who are unable (or unwilling) to give up their teaching positions to pursue full-time administrator training programs. Third, there is increasing recognition of the major limitations that exist with regard to full-time paid administrative internships.

The compromise followed in many programs is the use of a somewhat less structured field-based learning activity for aspiring administrators, generally referred to as a *planned field experience*. Here, the student of school administration who is employed on a full-time basis participates in activities that will allow him or her to practice the skills and techniques that are required of full-time administrators on the job. Although they are significantly more limited than the traditional internship, planned field experiences do enable people at least to see bits and pieces of the world of school administration. Aspiring administrators might, for example, work side by side with principals in developing a master schedule for the following school year, or they might sit in to watch parent conferences or other similar activities normally carried out by administrators. Such planned field experiences may be elective courses taken by students of administration or, more probably, state-mandated required activities for those seeking certification.

Whatever the motivation might be for people to engage in planned field experiences, it is clear that such activities have value for aspiring administrators. They are not replacements for the total immersion offered by the full-time internship, but they have the advantage of being an alternative learning experience that is available to the future administrator who must maintain full-time employment or who cannot obtain any special support from a school district for an internship. Planned field experiences are usually designed to allow the student to teach his or her normal load of courses and, during preparation periods or before or after the normal school day hours, to engage in activities of an administrative nature. In this way, people are still exposed to activities and duties carried out by practicing administrators so that they can gain some of the skills and insights they may need when they assume full-time administrative positions. School systems also benefit when teachers participate in planned field experiences because they gain additional sets of hands to carry out some tedious but much-needed work in school systems—work that might include the review of policy manuals, follow-ups on truant and tardy students, and home visits.

There are some significant limitations inherent in planned field experiences. Probably the greatest of these is that they provide, at best, only quick, snapshot views of the life of school administrators. Unlike the full-time internship, which puts the future leader into the "hot seat" (or, at least, a "warm seat") for a brief time, the field experience never fully takes the teacher out of the classroom to discover what it is really like to be "the boss." Descriptions of the value of field-based learning have traditionally suggested at least three benefits from this approach:

1. They give people the ability to acquire certain technical skills before going on the job for the first time.
2. They represent a way for people to learn more about a particular job so that they can test personal commitment to a career change.
3. They offer ways for important change to be introduced into schools as new people (with new ideas) are able to interact with existing staff.

Unfortunately, most of these benefits will not be achieved through the implementation of part-time planned field experiences in schools. In these settings, students typically will not be exposed to a full range of administrative activities so that they can acquire new skills. Second, such a brief exposure to administration provides little real opportunity for people to engage in the type of personal reflection that will enable them to ascertain levels of personal commitment to a new career. Third, short-term field experiences are never established in a way that encourages participants to blend into the ongoing social system of a school. The individual aspiring administrator will likely have no impact on the practices or procedures in the school system. In short, field experience participants are not likely candidates for the job of change agent.

Course-Embedded Experiences

The third approach frequently utilized is the incorporation of field-based learning activities within university courses. Examples of such efforts might include requiring students to carry out interviews of practicing administrators or attend school board meetings, or asking that students participate in a "community walk" or conduct local public opinion surveys. Other strategies in this vein involve inviting practicing administrators to make presentations in courses, or requiring students to carry out small-scale research projects in local schools.

All efforts to increase linkages between material presented in traditional classroom-based academic preparation programs and what goes on in the real world of schools are worthy of support, and most activities that are field-based and course-embedded fall into that category. When used properly, course-embedded field experiences serve to reinforce basic concepts and practices described apart from daily school situations. For example, a professor teaching a course in school–community relations will find no words that will describe the reality of the way parents living in poverty perceive the public schools any more accurately than a number of face-to-face interviews between students and the parents themselves. For many aspiring administrators, merely walking down a street in the inner city—an activity that might be assigned as part of the requirements in a structured, traditional course—may be a significant learning experience. In general, the greatest value of such a course-embedded learning activity is that it may enhance the value of instruction.

On the other hand, course-embedded field activities have often been abused by university instructors who view these experiences simply as a way to avoid the need to prepare a full complement of lectures for a term. Consider, for example, the number of guest speakers invited to speak to students in many graduate-level courses in educational administration. Often, such events amount to little more than bringing in local administrators to chat about their own biases by sharing "war stories" with students. It is our view that field-based learning activities, whether as stand-alone programs or as parts of existing courses, will never truly improve the quality of preservice preparation programs for school administrators unless they are well designed, focused, and clearly related to a broader set of instructional objectives. In short, field-based programs serve only as window dressing unless the designers of the programs have a vision of what they are trying to accomplish in the area of professional preservice preparation and development.

Summary

In this chapter we reviewed another component of professional development for school administrators. We looked at field-based learning experiences as a way to guide the preservice preparation of future school leaders.

We noted that such activities, if used properly, can serve to improve the quality of preservice programs. We also noted that, if preservice programs were to rely too heavily on such activities, it would likely decrease overall program effectiveness. Too great a reliance on apprenticeship models can be unduly restrictive of efforts to prepare leaders who will ultimately work to improve systems through change, rather than by merely maintaining the status quo as survivors. Field-based programs are valuable only if they avoid the temptation to show newcomers "how we do it around here," without giving an opportunity to construct better ways of "doing it."

The chapter concluded with a presentation of some of the more promising present and emerging practices designed to increase the opportunities for aspiring administrators to learn by doing. These strategies included the use of full-time administrative internships, planned field experiences for part-time students, and course-embedded learning activities designed to increase the opportunities for students enrolled in more traditional university courses to have some type of meaningful contact during their formal learning programs. Strengths and weaknesses associated with each of these programs were noted.

References

Achilles, Charles M. (1987). *Unlocking some mysteries of administration and administrators: A reflective perspective.* Unpublished briefing paper presented to the National Commission on Excellence in Educational Administration.

Baltzell, D. C., & Dentler, R. A. (1983). *Selecting American school principals: A sourcebook for educators.* Washington, DC: Abt Associates for the National Institute of Education.

Berliner, David. (1984). Making the right changes in preservice teacher education. *Phi Delta Kappan, 66,* 2:94–96.

Cornett, Lynn M. (1983). *The preparation and selection of school principals.* Atlanta: Southern Regional Education Board.

Cruickshank, Donald, & Armaline, William. (1986, October). Field experiences in teacher education: Considerations and recommendations. *Journal of Teacher Education, 37,* 3:34–40.

Daresh, John C., & LaPlant, James C. (1985, October). *Field relations in educational administration training programs.* Paper presented at the annual meeting of the Midwestern Educational Research Association, Chicago.

Daresh, John C., & Pape, Sharon. (1987, October). *Internships and other field experiences in the preparation of administrators and other professional educators.* Paper presented at the annual meeting of the Midwestern Educational Research Association, Chicago.

Dewey, John. (1938). *Education and experience.* New York: Macmillan.

Goodlad, John. (1984). *A place called school.* New York: McGraw-Hill.

Holloway, George E., & Morgan, Thomas D. (1967). *A final report to the Ford Foundation of the Inter-University Program Project II: The administrative internship in education.* Joint report published by the State University of New York at Buffalo, Cornell University, the University of Rochester, and Syracuse University.

Griffiths, Daniel, Stout, Robert, & Forsyth, Patrick. (Eds.). (1988). *Leaders for tomorrow's schools.* Berkeley, CA: McCutchan.

LaPlant, James C. (1988, January). *Future trends in administrator preparation.* Paper presented at a symposium for the Danforth Principals' Program candidates at The Ohio State University, Columbus.

Newell, Clarence A. (1952). What is an internship? *School and Society, 74,* 3: 358–360.

Peterson, Kent D. (1985). Obstacles to learning from experience and principal training. *Urban Review, 17,* 3:189–200.

Trump, J. L. (1971). *A school for everyone.* Reston, VA: National Association of Secondary School Principals.

Zeichner, Kenneth. (1985). The sociology of field experiences: Toward an understanding of the role of field experiences in teacher development. In L. Katz & J. Raths (Eds.), *Advances in teacher education* (Vol. 3). Norwood, NJ: Ablex.

CHAPTER FOUR

Personal and Professional Formation

The traditional approach followed in the preservice preparation of school administrators is relatively simple. After a few years of teaching experience, a person enrolls in a graduate program at a local university. In addition to receiving a master's degree, the aspiring administrator, with careful planning (so as not to take "too many" courses), completes the requirements for an entry-level administrative certificate. In many cases, the graduate program is in the field of educational administration, although it is common for people to pursue degrees in elementary or secondary education, curriculum and instruction, social studies education, or any one of many other different academic fields while also taking the proper courses prescribed by the state department of education or the university as the requirements for receiving an endorsement as a school administrator. This approach has normally been a comfortable one for students because the hurdles to administration are clearly indicated: Take X number of courses, file an application, and become certified (if not always qualified). Then, go look for a job—maybe. Universities have tended to like this model, too. Whenever competency and certification for a job can be satisfied by enrolling in courses, it keeps lecture halls filled and professors employed.

Happily or unhappily, depending on one's point of view, it was recognized long ago in many states that something beyond the completion of campus-based graduate courses in school administration was needed to help people as they prepared to take on principalships and superintendencies. Getting all A's and B's on a university transcript did not really prepare a person to serve as a school administrator. In addition to traditional coursework, it is recognized that people need some type of practical, field-based learning. As a consequence, more and more states have mandated the kinds of learning experiences that we described in Chapter 3. Students have tended to like this because it was a way to reduce the number of formal courses required for certification by doing some things that might be a bit more lively (and interesting) than the activities associated with conventional courses. They could learn about administration from "real people" out in the "real world." For the most part, universities have not been too upset with these new demands. After all, internships and planned field experiences have been classified as university credit-bearing activities. As such, they generate tuition and keep professors busy.

An important ingredient missing from most programs designed to prepare school administrators is personal and professional formation, or an effort to provide activities consciously directed toward helping people to synthesize learnings acquired through coursework (academic preparation) and field-based learning and, more important, to develop a personal appreciation of what it means to be an educational leader. As the research on beginning school administrators described in a later chapter indicates, a major problem faced by the novice is the lack of understanding of what leadership, authority, control, and power mean on an individual level. Formation may be seen as a way to address this problem while also providing a person with a way of constructing a personal moral and ethical stance to be used in framing responses to a wide variety of future administrative problems.

In this chapter, we look at the concept of personal and professional formation as an important part of a comprehensive program of professional development for school administrators. We begin by providing a definition of formation. Next, we review the five basic component elements of formation. We conclude the chapter with a consideration of the limitations that exist to using formation as part of professional development.

Definition of Formation

Personal and professional formation may be defined as the effort to enable an individual to become more aware of his or her own personal values and assumptions regarding the formal role of a school administrator. It is a time to consider one's personal commitment to the role of educational leader, and to decide the extent to which one is willing to make the changes that may be necessary to become an effective administrator. It is a time to reflect on one's personal definitions, sense of self, and moral and ethical stance regarding important educational issues.

Formation is not a new concept. It comes from the field of religious education, where it has long served as a central part of the strategy used to prepare individuals to assume roles as religious leaders. John Westerhoff (1987) of the Duke University Divinity School described formation as a process that "implies 'shaping' and refers to intentional, relational, experiential activities within the life of a story-formed faith community" (p. 581). He differentiates formation from other learning processes such as *education* (". . . 'reshaping' and refers to critical reflective activities related to these communal experiences," (p. 581) and *instruction* (". . . 'building' and refers to the means by which knowledge and skills useful to communal life are transmitted, acquired, and understood") (p. 581). Michael Warren (1987) extends this notion beyond the boundaries of religious education by observing that formation "is a central and inevitable process in all of human life" (p. 515) because it represents a way in which individuals are able to test some of their fundamental assumptions concerning beliefs and life-styles. It is, as Williams (1961) described in *The Long Revolution,* a time when people are able to learn "how to see" as they acquire an accurate means of understanding what is going on around them in the world:

> *One's version of the world one inhabits has a central biological function: it is a form of interaction with one's environment which allows a person to maintain life and to achieve greater control over the environment. . . . We "see" in certain ways—that is, we interpret sensory information according to certain rules— as a way of living. But these ways—these rules and interpretations—are, as a whole, neither fixed nor constant. We can learn new rules and new interpretations, as a result of which we shall literally see in new ways. (p. 18)*

Formation is an important part of the professional development of educational administrators for three reasons. First, as Westerhoff stated, it is a way in which individuals may come to understand themselves more completely. Second, it is a way to introduce a person to a broader understanding of the social realities of the world in which he or she must now work. Finally, we concur with Dykstra's (1987) assessment that formation may serve as the basis of the development of a collective culture, or congregation. We see this as an extremely important part of any effort to determine effective professional development strategies for school leaders, a group seeking greater opportunities to develop collegiality.

We do not wish to develop too many parellels between the preparation of future religious leaders and the professional development of educational administrators. There are, however, some rather obvious overlaps between the roles of school principal, for example, and church pastor, which make allusions to religious life and religious education appropriate in discussions of personal and professional formation in school settings.

Components of Formation

Five elements serve as components of our notion of formation: (1) mentoring, (2) personal reflection, (3) educational platform development, (4) appreciation of alternative styles, and (5) personal professional action planning.

Mentoring

Mentors drive personal and professional formation by serving as the people able to give administrators the type of feedback necessary to propel their professional development. It is not difficult for an administrator to engage in infrequent and isolated activities, but it is considerably more difficult for a person to sustain that growth and development over time. The use of mentoring relationships is one way to increase the likelihood that professional development will become a process and not merely an event.

We address the concept of mentoring in considerable detail in Chapter 10. Here we note simply that professional development programs for administrators might include mentors—experienced local administrators who are willing to provide advice and counsel to aspiring and practicing administrators—as a regular feature. These individuals would be more than field supervisors who work with students of administration during internships, or as evaluators of practicing administrators. In addition to serving as positive role models, mentors would be trained to provide needed psychosocial support to educational leaders. In this way, the emphasis in ongoing mentoring would be on the promotion of personal and professional formation, not simply the survival of administrators.

Models of such positive and ongoing mentoring systems are found in the newly emerging work of the National Association of Secondary School Principals Mentor Project, and also in the field of religious education, where individuals are assigned to seminarians as "spiritual advisors."

Personal Reflection

A second important component of the formation dimension is related to skills associated with personal reflection to guide administrators' performance. Reflection about one's professional performance in a role is a rather simple concept to define. As Posner (1985) observed concerning the use of reflectivity in student teaching, people would benefit greatly from their experiences if they had the opportunity to prepare for and think about those experiences before and after they occur. This theme has been championed by Schön (1983), who has often advanced the concept of reflection as a guide to action in many professions. The effective, reflective practitioner would be the person who realizes that, before he or she tries to solve problems, it is crucial to decide on the nature of the "right" problems to be solved.

In the professional development of educators, there has been a consistent recent call for emphasizing reflection for teacher candidates. As we noted in discussing the limitations of field-based learning in Chapter 3, such opportunities are not likely to achieve much of their promise if they are not guided properly. In an analysis of one of the drawbacks to present student teaching practices, Beyer (1984) observed that teaching candidates often learn negative behaviors in the field because they are prone to engage in "uncritical acceptance" of what they see, hear, and experience. The same danger exists in training programs for administrators, who may see wholly unacceptable or even unethical practices being rewarded in reality. Reflection, particularly if directed and guided by a sensitive mentor, is a powerful way to encourage the aspiring administrator to make critical judgments about the appropriateness of activities witnessed in the field. Again, referring to Beyer (1984):

> *Experiences which promote uncritical replication of observed practice are antithetical to the purposes of education itself. Promoting activities . . . which generate such perspective is, thus,*

contradictory to some fundamental purpose of education as this is often understood.

Developing reflective skill is one way to foster a spirit of questioning regarding the value of certain practices and assumptions seen in the field. This is a critical part of developing a personal professional identity.

Questions that may be used to guide the process of personal reflection and help a person to focus on what leadership is all about might include any or all of the following:

— What have I seen out in the field?
— How does what I have seen fit my personal view of what life as an administrator should be?
— Why is what I have learned important?
— What have I learned?
— How can I describe what I have seen?
— In what ways can I verify my description of what I have seen?
— What is the meaning of my experience?
— How does the description and my personal meaning relate to my personalized vision of what "should" be?
— What else can I learn?
— What is the overall significance of what I have done and seen?
— Now that I have done something, so what?

As the administrator proceeds through experiences followed by a period of reflecting on the answers to questions like these, he or she will develop a much deeper understanding of administration. Another benefit of this process is that, as a result of personalized reflection, a person can make a deliberate decision to leave administration or perhaps not to go into it in the first place. That, too, would be a desirable outcome, as it may reduce the number of people who pursue careers in administration "accidentally" or out of some false sense of purpose, rather than as a result of a conscious, deliberate plan and design.

Personal reflection might be integrated into an administrator preparation program or into any aspect of professional development through an expectation that candidates for future administrative positions, as well as practicing administrators, will keep a kind of diary, or reflective log, in which they regularly record personal descriptions of reality. Writing observations down in a formal way is important because it develops skills at articulating important personal beliefs.

Educational Platform Development

Another ingredient of formation is the preparation of a formal statement of one's own educational philosophy, beliefs, and values. Sergiovanni and Starratt (1988) referred to this as the development of a personalized educational platform. In their view, every professional educator should take the time to review personal stances about important educational issues. In doing this, a person would state the ideas that he or she espouses, in a way similar to the platform statements made by candidates running for a political office. The major difference would be that the educational platform should be designed to communicate a person's attitudes, values, and beliefs about education, even if these statements were contrary to the sentiments of the majority of members of the public.

Sergiovanni and Starratt suggest that an educational platform might include personalized responses to questions that come from the following ten major issues:

1. The aims of education
2. Major achievements of students
3. The social significance of student learning
4. The image of the learner
5. The value of the curriculum
6. The image of the teacher
7. The preferred kind of pedagogy
8. The primary language of discourse to be used in the learning situation
9. The preferred kinds of teacher–student relationships
10. The preferred kind of school climate

There are no absolutely correct or incorrect answers on any of these issues. However, the process of spending time to think through and write out a personal interpretation of each item has a number of advantages, particularly for the person moving into a new professional role. For one thing, preparing a platform statement helps in the process of formation by enabling a person to recognize strong beliefs (and perhaps unwanted biases as well) about significant issues in professional education. Some of the responses to the ten areas will come about much more quickly than will others. It is likely that these areas serve as place holders for concepts where there is probably the strongest allegiance to certain values. The basis of these may be viewed as the individual's core or nonnegotiable values. A second benefit is that this process may alert the individual to probable conflicts that are likely to lie ahead during a professional career. In addition to individual platforms, organizations also subscribe, at least implicitly, to strong statements of public values, usually stated as institutional philosophies and mission statements. When a person enjoys a deep understanding of an educational platform, it may be possible to determine in advance where sources of conflict are to be found in future relationships within an organization. Understanding the sources of probable value disputes should help most individuals find more effective ways of dealing with life in institutions.

One activity recommended as part of formation involves the expectation that every aspiring, beginning, or practicing administrator will take the time periodically to articulate as clearly as possible a personal educational platform in the way described here. There is also considerable value in sharing this platform statement with others, such as a mentor and other colleagues. This sharing process, which should take place frequently as a person's platform begins to emerge, is helpful in enabling others to gain insights into behavior and, perhaps even more important, in causing the individual to be as clear as possible about the nature of his or her personal values and beliefs.

One final comment concerning platform development is that a platform is something that is never completed. Rather, platform preparation must be viewed as a dynamic, ongoing activity carried out by every thoughtful school administrator.

One place where the development and articulation of educational platforms have been incorporated into a formal professional development program for administrators is in the preservice program offered by Indiana University at Indianapolis, in conjunction with the Danforth Foundation (Barnett & Brill, 1989). Every individual aspiring to hold an administrative position is expected to develop a personal educational platform that indicates his or her major assumptions and beliefs regarding leadership and effective schools. This document then serves as the foundation for all future learning activities, both in the university classroom and out in the field.

Understanding Interpersonal Styles

Another aspect of formation deals with developing an appreciation of different interpersonal styles in others and of how those differences relate to one's own style. A critical skill needed by every successful administrator is an appreciation for individual differences, along with a recognition that those differences may have a profound effect on the administrator's ability to exercise a preferred mode of behavior. This is important in several areas in which the administrator must work: in daily communication and ongoing relationships with staff and students, in the creation of teams (both teaching and management), and in school–community relations. In each case, the educational administrator must be sensitive to the dynamics that take place in school organizations when people behave differently from one another.

Merrill and Reid (1981) suggested that the appreciation of personal styles is a basic step in developing more effective performance in any professional role. Their work is based on these assumptions:

1. People perform most effectively when they are engaged in positive interpersonal relationships.
2. A mutually productive relationship is an asset that one needs to work at in order to maintain over time.
3. Modifying one's approach in order to improve an interpersonal relationship does not indicate a lack of sincerity or a Machiavellian desire to manipulate other people. To the contrary, it demonstrates respect for another person's right to be unique.
4. One of the greatest insights in life is the mature recognition that others are at least as important as oneself in the larger scheme of things.
5. Developing a wide variety of skills and techniques for handling interpersonal relationships is a highly desirable objective.
6. A certain amount of effort is required to develop new skills, and this effort is good in the sense that it represents a type of intense personal growth.
7. Those things that are out of one's control may be attributed to any source one desires, but controlling what can be controlled—one's own activities and actions—need not contradict one's beliefs and personal platform.

The suggestion that a school administrator should learn how to appreciate and understand interpersonal styles is an important complement to the idea of platform development. A well-developed professional development program for school administrators would do well to include formal training in the analysis of interpersonal styles and psychological types (Coulson, 1987).

Personal Professional Action Planning

The final component of formation is the articulation of a statement regarding one's overall personal professional development. This activity involves putting all of the insights gathered from the first two dimensions (academic preparation and field-based learning) together with insights derived from the activities of mentoring, personal reflection, platform development, and interpersonal style analysis into a single action plan. Here, administrators (or future administrators) are encouraged to indicate where they believe additional work may improve their effectiveness. Synthesis of learning may occur. In addition, the most desirable objective of any learning activity—namely, the acceptance of control over learning by the learner—takes place. As a result, this may truly be seen as a pivotal moment in either a preservice preparation program or an induction program for beginning administrators because it is the point at which inexperienced school administrators are "cut loose" from the preparation program and told that they must take responsibility for learning what will make sense throughout a professional career.

Although personal professional action planning is seen as the culminating activity of a preparation or induction (entry-year) program, it should be woven in as a continuing part of a solid sequence of activities designed to address the professional development needs of all administrators. From the beginning of a future administrator's first university course, there should be an explicit statement of the need to accept personal responsibility for translating course content into individual action. In fact, each of the dimensions of the tridimensional model may be seen as occurring simultaneously with the other features of the model. Personal and professional formation must be taking place while academic preparation is going on, and field-based learning should be taking place to enhance academic learning and clarify formation.

A personal professional action plan might be seen as analogous to the Individual Education Plans (IEPs) developed by schools for individual students with special learning needs. The major difference is that the nature of the specified learning and professional development activities for practicing administrators would be stated by the administrators themselves and would include a wide array of learning activities to ensure that they stay in their field. An example of the mandate of such a practice by a state education agency is found in Maine, where the Department of Education now requires every practicing administrator, with or without previous experience, to develop and implement an Individual Professional Action Plan prior to applying for a renewal of an administrative certificate every five years.

Summary

In this fourth chaper, we provided information concerning the purpose and content of the third element of our tridimensional model for the professional development of school administrators. This dimension—personal and professional formation—was compared to the notion of spiritual formation as a part of the preparation activities required of individuals assuming roles in religious life. The purpose of this dimension is to help people gain greater depth of understanding of their personal values, attitudes, strengths, weaknesses, and overall commitment to the field of educational administration.

The component elements of formation were described. These included mentoring, personal reflection, educational platform development, development of an understanding of interpersonal styles, and individual professional action planning. It was noted that using these various activities as part of a comprehensive professional development program for aspiring and practicing school administrators represents a significant departure from traditional approaches, which have been limited to academic preparation and field-based learning.

Our stance here has been that the professional development of school administrators is in need of major improvement. People need new ways to learn about leadership in schools. We believe that serving as a school administrator will continue to be a rewarding job, though extremely difficult and demanding. As a result, there is a critical need for strategies to be discovered that will better prepare and sustain individuals for this job in the future. Formation has truly been an important missing ingredient.

References and Suggested Readings

Barnett, Bruce, & Brill, Art. (1989, April). *The Danforth Foundation Program for the Preparation of Principals at Indiana University*. Paper presented at the meeting of the Danforth Principals' Network, Norman, Oklahoma.

Beyer, Landon E. (1984, May–June). Field experience, ideology, and the development of critial reflectivity. *Journal of Teacher Education, 35,* 3: 36–41.

Coulson, Alan A. (1987). An approach to headship development through personal and professional growth. In M. Hughes (Ed.), *Emerging issues in primary education.* London: Falmer Press.

Daresh, John C. (1988, October). *Professional formation and a tridimensional approach to the preservice preparation of school administrators.* Paper presented at the annual meeting of the University Council for Educational Administration, Cincinnati, Ohio.

Dykstra, Craig. (1987, Fall). The formative power of the congregation. *Religious Education, 82,* 4: 530–546.

Kolb, David. (1976). *Learning style profile.* Englewood Cliffs, NJ: Prentice-Hall.

Merrill, David W., & Reid, Roger. (1981). *Personal styles and effective performance.* Radnor, PA: Chilton.

Myers, Isabel. (1962). *Manual: The Myers-Briggs Type Indicator.* Palo Alto, CA: Consulting Psychologists Press.

Posner, George J. (1985). *Field experience: A guide to reflective teaching.* New York: Longman.

Schon, Donald A. (1983). *The reflective practitioner: How professionals think in action.* New York: Basic Books.

Sergiovanni, Thomas J., & Starratt, Robert J. (1988). *Supervision: Human perspectives,* 4th ed. New York: McGraw-Hill.

Warren, Michael. (1987, Fall). Religious formation in the context of social formation. *Religious Education, 82,* 4: 515–528.

Westerhoff, John. (1987, Fall). Formation, education, and instruction. *Religious Education, 82,* 4: 578–591.

Williams, Raymond. (1961). *The long revolution.* New York: Columbia University Press.

CHAPTER FIVE

Finding Talented Leaders

In previous chapters, we described a conceptual model that might be implemented as a way to improve the quality of preservice preparation of school administrators. We suggested that leadership development might be improved markedly if efforts were made to find an appropriate balance among the elements of academic preparation, field-based learning, and personal and professional formation.

We believe that even with the adoption of the model, the most fundamental issue associated with the improvement of educational leadership must come from the fact that the improvement process begins with more effective raw material. During the past few years, we have discussed with superintendents across the nation some of the problems associated with the recruitment of people to leadership roles in education. What they have told us is that there is a critical need for new school leaders, but that superintendents are frustrated in their search because those who apply for jobs are not viewed as particularly well qualified. Further, superintendents say that they know that there are teachers and others currently working in their districts who would likely be effective administrators but are not interested in making such a career move. The issue addressed in this chapter is the identification of future effective school leaders. We begin by looking at some of the special problems associated with the identification of potential leaders. Next we describe some of the issues associated with the recruitment of talented people to the field of educational leadership. Finally, we describe some promising strategies that might be followed in response to these problems and issues.

Special Problems of Identification

The identification of future potential educational leaders begins with a clear understanding of the characteristics that are to be sought in those who would be effective. If we had a clear understanding of what effective school administrators are supposed to do, we could start to look for people who were able to demonstrate the needed characteristics. The identification of individuals who should move into leadership roles would be a relatively simple task.

The problem is that most people do not have a clear notion of what they expect of school leaders. The current image of the principalship suggests that effectiveness is tied to a person's ability to serve as "instructional leader." There are two fundamental problems with this description. First, the term *instructional leadership,* though widely used, is rarely understood. Other than the fact that principals who serve as instructional leaders are somehow expected to spend more time engaged in reviewing and intervening in the teaching and learning activities of schools, there are only rare concrete descriptions in the literature of what constitutes desirable behavior for administrators. Researchers are working to define instructional leadership more precisely. Liu (1984) provided this definition:

> *Instructional leadership consists of direct or indirect behaviors that significantly affect teacher instruction and, as a result, student learning. (p. 33)*

Liu divided the tasks of instructional leadership behavior into two categories—direct and indirect. In broad terms, we might classify under direct leadership such activities as staff development and teacher supervision and evaluation, and under indirect leadership such activities as instructional facilitation, resource acquisition and building maintenance, and student problem resolution.

Another problem with the move toward acceptance of instructional leadership behavior as a desirable ideal for administrative behavior is that in the real world there are too many schools where it is clear that service as an instructional leader is not prized as the primary behavior sought by those who hire future principals and other leaders. There continue to be many apparent contradictions between stated school goals and the abilities and backgrounds of those who are selected to lead schools toward those goals. In many cases, principals are hired because of their ability to discipline students or to work effectively with parent and other community groups, or for many other reasons that are not part of a vision of effective instructional leadership.

We are not necessarily suggesting that any of these situations are better or worse than situations in which people are hired specifically because of their instructional expertise. Our purpose here is to point out the absence of any consensus in schools as to what "effective" leadership should be. This lack of consensus makes it quite difficult to develop any consistent way of deciding which individuals should or should not be actively identified and recruited to serve as future school administrators.

If the lack of clarity concerning the most desirable image of a school administrator causes some practical problems for school systems that seek new leaders, that same issue also has an effect on individuals who may wish to pursue school leadership careers. When opportunities are presented to school personnel to move toward careers in administration, there is often a negative reaction. People without school administrative experience have negative perceptions and views of the role of the school administrator. Many highly qualified, competent, and talented teachers dismiss careers in administration because they do not want to sit in an office all day, hassle teachers, discipline students, work with unhappy parents, or push paper—all activities frequently equated with the stereotypical role of the school administrator. Many people do not consider the fact that alternative images of school leadership are possible. Until some of those alternatives become better accepted and understood, we may continue to face the problem of individuals pre-screening themselves from administration, despite the realities of the job.

Recruitment Issues

One issue that continues to be a major concern related to the pre-service preparation of school administrators relates to the problem of recruiting talented individuals to serve as educational leaders. In the past, it was relatively easy to attract teachers into the ranks of school administrators because educators saw administration as a normal part of career advancement. Traditionally, if teachers wanted to earn more money, achieve higher status, or earn greater respect, they would leave the classroom and move toward a principalship or some other administrative role.

This image of administration as a normal extension of one's work as a teacher no longer exists. Teachers no longer see administration as a way to improve their salaries, prestige, or respect among other colleagues. The pay differential that formerly existed between teaching and administration is no longer as pronounced as it was a few years ago. In many states, average teacher salaries are above $30,000 per year, whereas administrative pay is often maintained at about $40,000 per year. The difference, of course, is that, for the additional $10,000, the administrator works for at least eleven months a year instead of ten, works many evenings, and deals with an enormous amount of stress brought on by community members, other administrators, school board members, parents, students, and teachers.

These figures are all based on average pay scales. In truth, many of the best candidates for administrative posts are teachers with advanced degrees and many years of professional experience. In such cases, it is not unusual to find classroom teachers being paid well beyond $50,000, while principals in the same district might actually earn less, with more hours of assigned duties.

Thus, it is becoming increasingly difficult to attract the "best and the brightest" people to go into the field of educational administration. Financial rewards do not exist to the extent that they may have in the past, and the general perception among many people, including teachers, is that the life of the school administrator is anything but one that will lead to greater prestige and respect.

The problems with recruitment of future administrators are related to concerns associated with getting individuals to think about leadership roles. When these concerns are also associated with the enduring issue of attempting to attract underrepresented groups—women and minorities—into administrative roles in schools, the problems of recruitment are made even more acute. There is an imbalance between the gender and racial backgrounds of the majority of present-day school administrators and the student populations they serve. Increasingly, the combined minority student population of public school systems represents a majority of all students. Female students make up at least half the student enrollments, if not the faculty populations, in most schools. However, the ranks of school administrators still consist largely of white males.

Two distinct problems need to be addressed with regard to the recruitment of more educational leaders who will make a positive difference in schools. The first concerns the issue of making the field of educational leadership more desirable in the eyes of prospective leaders. Current popular images of the school administrator as little more than a student disciplinarian and building manager must be changed, or at least an image must be created that suggests that newcomers to the field of administration will have the opportunity to carve out their roles differently. We believe that many good people are being kept from entering leadership roles because they see such roles as contrary to their own personal visions of the primary activities of educators. School systems that are seriously interested in attracting high-quality candidates for administrative roles need to reexamine their expectations for administrative duties to determine if these descriptions are so narrow that they prevent some good people from joining the field.

The second problem concerning the recruitment of quality educators into leadership roles is the fact that such recruitment efforts must be proactive. It is no longer sufficient for school districts simply to sit back and wait for people to decide that they might want to go into administration someday. Instead, school systems that wish to have access to a pool of talented individuals who might be called upon to fill future leadership roles must take steps to "grow their own" talent. Teachers and other staff members who give evidence of having leadership potential need to be encouraged by superintendents and other administrators to think about going into school administration as a career. The days of expecting large numbers of teachers to go out for administrative training, followed by an expectation that at least some of these individuals will eventually surface as strong candidates for leadership openings, are coming to an end. School systems need to identify promising individuals and nudge them into administration by providing released time for training, special learning activities to support on-the-job learning, and even financial incentives.

With regard to the concern for the recruitment of women and minority group representatives into the field of educational leadership, we suspect that even more forceful efforts at proactive recruitment need to be discovered. It may not be enough simply to try to find future minority administrators from among the ranks of the present teaching staff. Districts may need to go well beyond their present staffs to find talented individuals. We suspect that such recruitment may have to begin while individuals are still enrolled as undergraduates in arts and sciences programs or in other noneducation fields in universities. The proactive recruitment of minority candidates for leadership roles may have to begin even earlier, when students are still enrolled in high school or even in junior high school. Career counseling for many fields often begins at such early stages. But when was the last time a local or state school administrators' group—or any agency, for that matter—sponsored an information booth at a high school career day? Many private industries do so, health care agencies do so, and even teacher associations and teacher education institutions attempt to "sell" their line of work to young clients. Yet school leadership is rarely forged from similar efforts to attract young aspirants. As a result, we are often dismayed at the results of recruitment that is anything but a proactive process. School administration may indeed be one of the most significant roles in society, yet entrance into it as a career is more often than not a function of happenstance.

Some Promising Directions

Despite some of the shortcomings and problems that we have identified in the area of administrator identification, recruitment, and selection, there are some indications that a few things currently happening in the field hold some potential for improving the status quo.

Perhaps the most significant movement toward finding more effective ways of determining the quality of the future talent pool of school administrators has been the development and utilization of assessment center procedures in a growing number of settings. This strategy suggests that a set of research-based characteristics related to effectiveness in managerial positions has been identified, and that there are techniques that may be used to determine whether or not a particular individual possesses those characteristics. In recent years the National Association of Secondary School Principals (NASSP) has taken the lead in promoting the concept of assessment centers as a way to identify probable successful future educational leaders.

According to the NASSP assessment center model, sixteen skill areas have been identified to serve as the basis of a composite vision of leadership. The identified skill areas are as follows:

1. *Problem analysis:* The ability to seek out relevant data and analyze complex information to determine the important ele-

ments of a problem situation; searching for information with a purpose.

2. *Judgment:* The ability to reach logical conclusions and make high-quality decisions based on available information; skill in identifying educational needs and setting priorities; the ability to evaluate communications critically.

3. *Organizational ability:* The ability to plan, schedule, and control the work of others; skill in using resources in an optimal fashion; the ability to deal with a volume of paperwork and heavy demands on one's time.

4. *Leadership:* The ability to get others involved in solving problems; the ability to recognize when a group requires direction and to interact effectively with a group in order to guide them in accomplishing a task.

5. *Sensitivity:* The ability to perceive the needs, concerns, and .personal problems of others; tact in dealing with persons from different backgrounds; the ability to deal effectively with people concerning emotional issues; knowledge of what information to communicate and to whom.

6. *Decisiveness:* The ability to recognize when a decision is required (disregarding the quality of the decision) and to act quickly.

7. *Range of interests:* Competence in discussing a variety of subjects—education, politics, current events, economics, and the like; active participation in events.

8. *Personal motivation:* The need to achieve in all activities; evidence that work is important to one's personal satisfaction; the ability to be self-policing.

9. *Educational values:* Possession of a well-reasoned educational philosophy.

10. *Stress tolerance:* The ability to perform under pressure and despite opposition; the ability to think on one's feet.

11. *Oral communication:* The ability to make clear oral presentations of facts or ideas.

12. *Written communication:* The ability to express ideas clearly in writing and to write appropriately for different audiences—students, parents, and others.

13. *Conflict management:* The willingness to intervene in conflict situations and the ability to develop solutions that are agreeable to all persons involved.

14. *Political astuteness:* The ability to perceive critical features of the environment, such as power structure, principal players,

and special interest groups, and to formulate alternatives that reflect realistic expectations.

15. *Risk taking:* The extent to which calculated risks are taken on the basis of sound judgments.
16. *Creativity:* The ability to generate ideas that provide new and different solutions to management problems or opportunities.

The items that form the basis of the assessment center technology should be used only to guide broad screening of candidates for administrative positions. They should not be used in an absolute sense as a way to bar individuals from moving forward with their aspirations to serve as educational leaders. We believe that assessment centers are good diagnostic devices. They may be useful ways to give people feedback concerning their strengths and weaknessnes as future school administrators.

The second positive development related to the identification and recruitment of future talented leaders is found in many local efforts to become more proactive with such efforts. In a large number of school systems across the nation, there have been many attempts to cultivate leadership talent from within. This has traditionally been done by offering special leadership preparation programs for aspiring administrators who have been identified or tapped by the system. In recent years, such programs also have served as ways to attract women and minority candidates to move into administration. Deliberate leadership recruitment programs must be started in districts across the nation as a way to promote the entrance of more qualified leaders to education.

Summary

In this chapter, we looked at the issue of how to identify better qualified individuals for recruitment into school administration. We also considered ways of recruiting those who have been identified as strong candidates. One of the most important specific issues that we examined was the need to find more representatives of underrepresented groups for recruitment into school leadership roles.

We believe that the identification and recruitment of future educational leaders cannot be left to chance. If schools are to improve, then leadership must improve. Leadership will not improve unless there is a consistent image of the responsibility that all educators have in attracting better qualified individuals to seek careers as educational leaders.

Reference

Liu, Ching-Jen. (1984). *An identification of instructional leadership behaviors of effective high school principals.* Unpublished Ed.D. dissertation, University of Cincinnati.

CHAPTER SIX

Lessons from Teacher Education

Efforts to reform education in the United States have focused on changing the ways in which professional educators are prepared to assume their roles. Although at least two recent groups—the National Commission on Excellence in Educational Administration and the National Policy Board for the Preparation of School Administrators—have worked to reform administrative preparation, most efforts to find more effective ways to prepare educators have looked at the role of the classroom teacher.

In this chapter, we review some of the major recommendations related to the improvement of teacher education in the United States. On the basis of that review, we examine some of the most powerful potential applications of teacher education reform, if utilized in programs designed to prepare future educational administrators. We conclude by noting that, although it is possible to apply some recommendations from teacher education to the preparation of school administrators, there are some features of the role of the educational administrator that make the issues involved quite different from those that need to be faced as part of teacher education.

Current Issues in Teacher Education

Efforts to promote significant changes in the ways in which teachers are prepared in this country are best noted through a brief review of the major recommendations presented in reform reports of the past few years. In particular, we focus on the recommendations made by the Holmes Group and the Carnegie Forum, two efforts that have served as visible examples of reform programs during the past five years.

The Holmes Group

In 1984 the deans of the colleges of education at a relatively small number of large, research-oriented universities formed a compact that was directed toward changing the structure of teacher education institutions. This consortium, which has taken its name from Henry W. Holmes, dean of the Harvard Graduate School of Education in the 1920s, devoted its efforts to elevating the status and quality of teacher education across the nation.

Michael Sedlak (1987, pp. 315–317) of Michigan State University has synthesized the major points of the Holmes Group, which appeared in a document known as *Tomorrow's Teachers*. He noted that the group has centered its suggestions for reform on five basic proposals:

1. Make the education of teachers more intellectually sound by expecting prospective teachers to become thoughtful students of the improvement of teaching. This would require major reform of instruction in undergraduate liberal arts and sciences coursework, in coursework related to pedagogy, and in preprofessional clinical experiences. As a result, the professional preparation of teachers will shift from an undergraduate to a graduate-level focus.

2. Recognize differences in teachers' knowledge, skills, and commitment, and in their education, certification, work, and career opportunities by distinguishing among novices (instructors), competent professional teachers (professional teachers), and high-level professional leaders (career professionals). It is also recommended that strategies be developed to promote differentiated staffing or role responsibilities in schools.

3. Create standards of entry to the profession, such as examinations and educational requirements, that are professionally relevant and intellectually defensible.

4. Connect institutions of higher education to schools in order to make better use of expert teachers and to build appropriate demonstration sites where new career opportunities, working conditions, and administrative arrangements might be developed and refined.

5. Make schools better places for teachers to work and for

students to learn by altering professional roles and responsibilities for teachers.

Although the Holmes Group has attracted membership from nearly seventy institutions at one time or another during the past seven years, its work has not escaped considerable criticism.

First, a common observation concerns the authenticity of Holmes Group member institutions' commitment to the reform of teacher education in the first place. The majority of universities involved with the initial Holmes proposal are large, research-oriented institutions that have not been perceived as historically having had a visible commitment to preservice teacher education. Absent from the list of participating universities have been most normal schools across the nation—institutions that owe their roots to the field of teacher education. Critics have often pointed to this apparent contradiction as a reason to suspect the viability of the Holmes reform agenda.

A second set of criticisms have focused on the issue of the suggestions related to the "improvement of professionalism" as a way to ensure that teaching would be improved. Being a good teacher and being more professional are not necessarily overlapping concepts. Making modifications, such as requiring that individuals complete baccalaureate degrees prior to moving into professional education preparation, serves only as a symbolic improvement and does not address the foundation of what may be needed to improve the central technical activity of teaching.

Related to this criticism that Holmes suggests only symbolic improvement is an observation by Walter Feinberg (1987), who raised concerns regarding the value of restricting teachers to teaching only in the subject matter of their undergraduate majors. Feinberg noted (p. 366) that such a restriction only ". . . seems to inhibit the establishment of experimental, interdisciplinary programs by reinforcing departmental boundaries and legitimizing the view that lines between subject matter areas are fixed by some unbending law of nature."

Perhaps the most powerful set of arguments against the Holmes proposal concerns the belief that it will serve to screen out a large percentage of economically disadvantaged groups from moving into teaching by requiring that prospective teachers pursue advanced graduate degrees before taking their first teaching jobs. As a result, further barriers will be created to prevent minority representatives from pursuing careers in classrooms. In addition, the recommendation that different levels be created for beginning, experienced, and master teachers would encourage a caste system that would serve as little more than a disincentive to collegial teaching behavior rather than a reinforcement of that concept. Critics are quick to point at the research orientation of Holmes institutions as models of three-tiered professional worlds, wherein assistant professors pay homage to associate professors, who in turn revere (and aspire to) the level of full professor. Systems such as this do little to promote overall organizational effectiveness or excellence.

Finally, many note the impracticality of implementing much of what the Holmes Group suggests. For example, requiring all beginning teachers to possess advanced graduate degrees may appear to be an improvement. However, school district administrators have noted that it is hard to justify the expenditure of advanced salary levels reserved for teachers with master's degrees for first-year instructors who have yet to be tested in classrooms. Although Holmes calls for more sophisticated clinical experiences to prepare future teachers, such experiences are likely to serve as artificial substitutes for real school experiences.

Carnegie Forum

Shortly after the Holmes Group issued its recommendations for the improvement of teacher education, the Carnegie Foundation presented a number of suggestions for reforming the ways in which classroom educators are prepared.

In its summary report, *A Nation Prepared: Teachers for the 21st Century,* the Carnegie Forum developed a plan that included the following recommendations for ways of improving teaching in the United States (Carnegie Commission, 1986, pp. 55–56):

1. Create a National Board for Professional Teaching Standards, organized with a regional and state membership structure, to establish high standards for what teachers need to know and be able to do, and to certify teachers who meet the standard.
2. Restructure schools to provide a professional environment for teachers, freeing them to decide how best to meet state and local goals for children while holding them accountable for students' progress.
3. Restructure the teaching force, and introduce a new category

of "lead teachers" with the proven ability to provide active leadership in redesigning the schools and in helping their colleagues to uphold high standards of learning and teaching.

4. Require a bachelor's degree in the arts and sciences as a prerequisite for the professional study of teaching.

5. Develop a new professional curriculum in graduate schools of education leading to a master of teaching degree, based on systematic knowledge of teaching and including internships and residencies in the schools.

6. Mobilize the nation's resources to prepare minority youngsters for teaching careers.

7. Relate incentives for teachers to schoolwide student performance, and provide schools with the technology, services, and staff essential to teacher productivity.

8. Make teachers' salaries and career opportunities competitive with those in other professions.

Criticisms of the Carnegie Report are similar to those leveled against the Holmes Group work. Both assume that education will be improved if teaching is improved, and teaching will be improved if it can be made more "professional." Once again, professionalism is equated with technical performance, and that equation is questionable.

Teacher Education Reforms in Administrator Preparation

Recommendations for reform made by the Holmes Group, the Carnegie Forum, and other national and regional groups were directed at the improvement of teacher education programs. One must be cautious about trying to generalize too quickly to administrator preparation. Teacher education reformers suggest two important issues that need to be applied to the enhancement of programs for future school administrators: first, that preservice programs need to take into account more directly the needs of adult learners, and, second, that preservice preparation would be improved greatly if it was based on the development of individual reflection and self-analysis skills. In the next section, we look at some of the major assumptions in these two areas, and we consider their applications to the world of administrator preservice preparation.

Adult Learning

Intuition has long suggested that adults have different learning needs than children do. Malcolm Knowles (1970), a major contributor to the field of adult education, is generally credited with coining the word *andragogy* (the art and science of teaching adults) as distinct from *pedagogy* (the art and science of teaching children). Knowles identified four critical characteristics of adults and their patterns of learning:

1. As a person matures, his or her self-concept moves from one of dependency to one of self-direction.
2. The mature person tends to accumulate a growing reservoir of experience that provides a resource for learning.
3. The adult's readiness to learn becomes increasingly oriented toward the developmental tasks of his or her assigned social roles.
4. The adult's time perspective changes from postponed application of knowledge to immediate application, and, accordingly, his or her orientation toward learning shifts from subject-centeredness to problem-centeredness.

Knowles's work encouraged others to conduct research and write in the field of adult education, and some work is useful for us in seeking to improve the ways in which people are prepared to assume leadership roles in schools. Wood and Thompson (1980) reviewed some salient aspects of adult learning:

1. Adults learn when they consider the goals and objectives of a learning activity to be realistic, related, and important to a specific issue at hand.
2. Adults learn, retain, and use what they perceive as relevant to their immediate personal and professional needs.
3. Adults need to see the results of their efforts and have frequent and accurate feedback about progress that is being made toward their goals.
4. Adult learning is highly ego-involved. When a person is unsuccessful at a given learning task, it is likely that he or she will take this as an indication of personal incompetence and failure.
5. Adults always come to any learning experience with a wide range of previous experiences, knowledge, skills, and competencies.

6. Adults want to be the origins of their own learning, and they wish to be directly involved in the selection of learning objectives, content, activities, and so forth.
7. Adults tend to resist any learning experience that they believe is either an open or an implied attack on their personal or professional competence.
8. Adults reject prescriptions by others for their learning.
9. Adult motivation comes from the learner and not from any external source. Although this may generally be said of motivation of all individuals, it is true that, as a person matures, efforts to motivate from outside the individual will be less likely to succeed.

Taken together, these characteristics of adult learning should provide those who plan learning experiences for school administrators with some important insights into how such experiences should be planned and carried out. First, the fact that adults want (and learn best from) experiences that address immediate problems suggests that planners of professional development should make certain that what they do is directed toward addressing immediate, practical concerns faced by aspiring and practicing school leaders. Presentations of the latest research on instructional leadership, no matter how carefully prepared, will be exercises in futility unless administrators clearly understand how this research relates to what needs to be done now in their schools. There is a danger, however, in trying to narrow the professional development focus too directly to issues of immediate importance to a school or district; such a practice might be equally futile because adults tend to reject prescriptions—quick fixes—to complex problems. Those planning professional development for school administrators need to understand what the real problems are in a school or district and avoid the temptation to provide Band-Aid responses to current problems while ignoring more serious ones.

The study of adult learning, or andragogy, also provides some important clues about adult self-concept needs. Administrators often complain that professional development learning experiences seem threatening—that participants often feel incompetent. The implication is that as people become more mature and fixed in their ways, they become increasingly self-conscious in situations where they believe they might experience failure (and perhaps ridicule) in front of others. Professional development activities must therefore be planned so that administrators will not be put in situations where their performance might be compared publicly with that of their colleagues. Thus, we might question the wisdom of using activities such as role playing, which require people to "perform" by demonstrating particular techniques in front of others, especially when people have not clearly volunteered to do so.

Finally, the literature in adult learning shows that as people mature, they accumulate additional learning experiences, and that those who are involved with the design of these experiences should recognize the potential richness of this previous learning. Nothing is more frustrating than being asked to participate in activities designed to send everyone back to square one. Such practices not only ignore an important resource for teaching adults but also violate a basic rule of effective professional development, namely that individual differences among learners must be taken into account.

Reflection

Efforts to reform teacher education have pointed to the need to increase the number of opportunities for aspiring teachers to engage in a process of continuous reflection as they proceed toward attaining their professional goals. This emphasis is also valid as part of structured efforts to improve the ways people are made ready to assume leadership roles in schools as well.

Reflection about one's performance in a professional role is a rather simple concept to define. As Posner (1985) observed concerning the use of reflectivity in student teaching, people would benefit greatly from their experiences if they had the opportunity to prepare for and think about those experiences before and after they occur. This theme has been championed by Donald Schön (1983), who advanced the concept of reflection as a guide to action in many professions. Again, the concept is simply stated, namely that the effective, reflective practitioner would be the person who realizes that, before he or she tries to solve problems, it is critical to think about the nature of the "right" problems to be solved.

In the preservice preparation of educators, there has been a consistent call for adding reflection as a component for teacher candidates. Such opportunities are not likely to achieve their greatest promise if they are not guided. In an analysis of some of the drawbacks to student teaching, Beyer (1984) observed that teaching candidates often learn negative behaviors in the field because they are prone to engage in "uncritical acceptance" of what they see. The same danger, of course, exists in training programs for administrators, who may see wholly unacceptable or even unethical practices being rewarded in reality. Reflection is a way to encourage both aspiring and experienced administrators to make critical judgments about the appropriateness of activities witnessed in the field. Referring again to Beyer (1984),

> *Experiences which promote uncritical replication of observed practice are antithetical to the purposes of education itself. Promoting activities . . . which generate such perspective is, thus, contradictory to some fundamental purposes of education as this is often understood.*

Developing reflective skill is one important way to develop a sense of questioning regarding the value of certain practices and assumptions seen in the field, and this is a critical part of developing a professional identity.

Questions that may guide the process of personal reflection and help a person to focus on a sense of what leadership is all about might include the following:

— What have I seen out in the field?
— How does what I have seen fit my personal view of what life should be as an administrator?
— Why is what I have seen important?
— What have I learned?
— What do I want to know more about?
— How can I describe what I have seen?
— In what ways can I verify my description of what I have seen?
— What is the meaning of my experience?
— How does the description and my personal meaning relate to my personalized vision of what "should" be?
— What else can be learned?
— What is the overall significance of what I have done and seen?
— Now that I have done something, so what?

As administrators go about their busy schedules and reflect on answers to questions like these, they will develop a much deeper understanding of administration. Another benefit of this process is that personalized reflection will lead some people to make a deliberate decision not to stay in administration. That, too, may be a highly desirable result from time to time.

Differences between Administrators and Teachers

There are several fundamental differences between the roles of teacher and administrator. We have identified at least five characteristics of school administration that make it quite unlikely that any specific activities designed to improve the quality of preservice teacher preparation will have a similar value for another group of professional educators.

1. The research on administration is not clear enough to guide administrative development.

Recent research on teaching behavior has been comprehensive and relatively sophisticated, so that there now exists some clear descriptions of what teachers should do in their classrooms to promote more desirable student outcomes. Although we are certainly not at the place where precise blueprints and road maps are available to point the way toward every move that needs to be made by a future classroom teacher, there is a body of research that at least sheds some light on the types of things that seem to be done more often by effective teachers. In turn, this information can be used as the basis for providing guidance to beginners who seek direction concerning what they should do in their classrooms. These beginners seek validated and effective practices. Those involved with the preservice preparation of teachers, then, have some basis in research to help with the quality of contact that they have with learners. In short, the vision may be cloudy, but there is some notion of what "a good teacher" does on a daily basis.

By contrast, research on school administration has only recently started to examine the question of what specific behaviors by administrators seem to be more or less appropriate in terms of student outcomes. Traditionally, research in the field of educational administration has been directed at discovering interrelationships among organizational structures, activities, and policies. The essential issue explored has been "how" administration is carried out. With a few exceptions, such as James Lipham's classic analysis of the personalities of "effective" and "ineffective" principals more than thirty years ago (Lipham, 1960), it has only been within the last ten years that scholars have started to turn their attention to the identification of specific behaviors by administrators that are related to student learning. There has been a long history of research into the question. "What do effective teachers do?" But only a few researchers have started to ask, "What do effective principals do?" Too often, the sharing of folklore and the swapping of war stories ("The way I used to do it . . .") have served as the reservoir of knowledge shared by practicing school administrators.

The consequences of this lack of highly focused attention to precise administrative behavior patterns is clear with regard to preservice preparation programs. When there is little evidence of what good administrators ought to do, a handicap exists for those who would prepare colleagues of the future. Teacher educators know that beginning teachers will likely see more student success in their classes if direct instruction is used (at least under certain circumstances); more enthusiasm is demonstrated; and positive, pleasant, and optimistic attitudes and feelings are expressed by the teacher (Berliner & Tikunoff, 1976). Those who prepare future administrators would find it difficult, if not entirely impossible, to suggest that students will achieve greater success on standardized achievement tests if the principal has fewer meetings with the total teaching staff, dictates more letters, smiles more, or sees fewer parents during a school day. Progress is being made in looking into this issue. We know, for example, that principals should use the public address system only rarely, and that they should spend more time observing teachers in their classes. There is, however, a long way to go before the preparation of administrators is built upon a refined data base and the same kinds of clear descriptions that influence the preservice preparation of teachers.

2. "New" administrators are not new to schools.

The preservice preparation of classroom teachers is driven by the assumption that people enrolled in teacher education programs have relatively little previous experience as school employees. Only a small amount of time is actually spent in schools as part of preservice preparation programs. On occasion, one might find an aspiring teacher who used to work as an aide or in some other full-time capacity in schools. For the most part, however, teacher educators devote a considerable amount of time trying to show people what life in and around schools is all about. Every class, every student, and each parent interaction is a new adventure filled with potential learning or trauma for the beginning teacher.

The same is not true for beginning administrators. In most states, there is an expectation that administrative personnel will have spent from three to five years in a classroom before receiving an initial certificate. That amount of time does nothing to guarantee that an individual is sensitive to the multitude of demands that accompany an administrator's job. On the other hand, every person moving from the classroom to an administrative position at least knows what a school looks like, how students tend to behave, and what parents are likely to ask or demand. This is particularly true when one recalls the fact that many "beginning" principals have often had previous experience as lead teachers or in other leadership roles.

The person who prepares future administrators, therefore, is not so much an individual who must provide an initial orientation to the field of professional education or the world of schools, as he or she is a translator who can help the aspiring administrator learn a new dialect that is spoken in the same familiar land.

3. Administrators are formal leaders.

When people receive administrative assignments, they automatically take on positions of formal authority, power, and control of a school. An administrator is a formal leader who, in a sense, has been appointed by a local governing board to manage the district or a single school building. For many who take this job, the responsibility for providing leadership becomes one of "knowing all the answers" or, at least, never admitting publicly that one does not have all the right answers all the time. One can criticize this view as distorted, inaccurate, or just plain foolish. It is, however, a view that exists and is likely to persist. And it is one that makes the development of effective preservice preparation programs for school administrators exceedingly difficult.

The same difficulty occasionally arises in relation to the processes associated with the preparation of future classroom teachers. In the minds of many people, the image still exists that a teacher is paid to know everything, and that seeking the assistance of colleagues might in some way be perceived as a sign of weakness or even incompetence. For both the aspiring administrator and the aspiring teacher, preservice programs are effective only when they promote the understanding that seeking support and guidance from others in the organization is an action that ultimately promotes strength, not weakness.

4. Administrative "peers" usually are not equal to the beginner.

The establishment of open and honest communication and rapport between aspiring administrators and more experienced colleagues in the field is a goal that is quite difficult to achieve. Equal and nonjudgmental relationships often do not exist when experienced practitioners begin to work with newcomers. This is in contrast to the ways in which experienced classroom teachers often work openly and directly with beginning colleagues. It is not uncommon for student teachers to receive a considerable amount of assistance from their cooperating teachers. It is much less likely that the same would be true for a student of educational administration seeking support from an experienced practicing administrator.

These four issues that separate teacher preparation from administrator preparation do not always exist to the extent that we suggested here. For example, in some cases beginning administrators are not being prepared to move into the field as competitors to other administrators or as adversaries to the "labor force"— teachers. But strategies to prepare teachers will not always be effective as techniques used in the preservice education of school administrators.

Summary

The purpose of this chapter was to consider the potential overlaps that might exist between the well-developed knowledge base related to the preservice preparation of classroom teachers and programs designed to prepare future school administrators. We noted some of the recent reform efforts in the field of teacher education, namely the Holmes Group recommendations and the report of the Carnegie Forum on the Improvement of Teacher Education. Next, we looked at key ideas that are expressed in teacher education reform proposals and that appear to have considerable value as ingredients of more effective preservice preparation programs for school administrators. In particular, we considered the need to include greater appreciation of the learning needs of adults, and also to include a greater emphasis on the use of reflection as part of preservice preparation.

The chapter concluded with a review of four characteristics of school administration that interfere with the application of some of the most desirable techniques traditionally emphasized in teacher education programs. Our intent was to point to a number of places where it may be futile, if not simply unwise, to attempt to transfer teacher education improvement strategies directly to the preparation of school administrators.

References

Berliner, D., & Tikunoff, W. (1976). The California Beginning Teacher Evaluation Study: An Overview of the Ethnographic Study. *Journal of Teacher Education, 27,* 5:24–30.

Beyer, Landon E. (1984, May–June). Field experience, ideology, and the development of critical reflectivity. *Journal of Teacher Education, 35,* 3:36–41.

Carnegie Forum on the Improvement of Teacher Education. (1986). *A nation prepared: Teachers for the 21st century.*

Feinberg, Walter (1987). The Holmes Group report and the professionalization of teaching. In Jonas F. Soltis (Ed.), *Reforming teacher education: The impact of the Holmes Group report.* New York: Teachers College Press.

Holmes Group. (1986). *Tomorrow's teachers: A report of the Holmes Group.* East Lansing, MI: The Holmes Group.

Knowles, Malcolm S. (1970). *The modern practice of adult education.* New York: Association Press.

Lipham, James M. (1960). Personal variables of effective administrators. *Administrator's Notebook, 9,* 1:1–4.

Posner, George J. (1985). *Field experience: A guide to reflective teaching.* New York: Longman.

Schön, Donald A. (1983). *The reflective practitioner: How professionals think in action.* New York: Basic Books.

Sedlak, Michael W. (1987, Spring). Tomorrow's teachers: The essential arguments of the Holmes Group report. In Jonas F. Soltis (Ed.), *Reforming teacher education: The impact of the Holmes Group report.* New York: Teachers College Press.

Wood, Fred, & Thompson, Steven R. (1980). Guidelines for better staff development. *Educational Leadership, 37:*374–378.

CHAPTER SEVEN

Research on Beginning Administrators

There is a paradox in the area of the professional development of school administrators. On one hand, there is a general recognition of the importance of educational leaders, and an awareness that it is crucial that people moving into those roles for the first time enjoy successful experiences. On the other hand, there is a remarkable paucity of structured research on the topic of beginning administrators and their needs.

In this chapter, we consider the findings of recent studies of beginning school administrators. Our purpose is to consider the ways in which this information may be utilized to focus efforts to lead programs to assist inexperienced educational leaders. Such information can help in planning effective learning programs for those who have moved into the administrator's office for the first time.

Recent Research

Existing research on problems encountered by beginning administrators indicates that there is a major difference between the needs of teachers and those of school administrators. Traditionally, scholars have not spent much time looking at the issue of *how* people become administrators; instead, research has more typically been directed at *what* practicing administrators do—or are supposed to do—on the job. Despite this limitation on the quantity of data, some fairly strong statements related to how people move into administration emerge. Research concerning initial socialization to educational administration makes it clear that any type of support, such as formalized entry-year programs, would be welcome. But only sporadically have activities been designed to assist new administrators.

Among some of the recent investigations have been small-scale studies conducted by Nockels (1981) and Turner (1981), and doctoral research by Marrion (1983), Sussman (1985), and Diederich (1988). A common finding of these works, and also in a broader study by Daniel Duke (1988), has been that the administrative entry year may be best characterized as a time filled with anxiety, frustration, and self-doubt.

Another study was recently done in England by Weindling and Earley (1987). This project reviewed the characteristics of the first years of secondary school head teachers (principals) throughout the United Kingdom. Surveys and interviews were carried out to gain information from beginning principals, their teaching staffs, and their administrative superiors regarding the ways in which principals were frustrated in their new positions. Among the recommendations from this study was that beginning principals need to receive special consideration and support from their employing school systems. Weindling and Earley noted that a major problem for head teachers has been isolation from their peers. Some ways need to be found to reduce the sense of isolation that novice administrators tend to feel so strongly.

In a study of beginning principals in Ohio, Daresh (1986) found that administrators' concerns arise in three distinct areas: (1) problems with role clarification (understanding who they were, now that they were principals, and how they were supposed to make use of their authority); (2) limitations on technical expertise (how to do the things they were supposed to do, according to their job descriptions); and (3) difficulties with socialization to the profession and individual school systems (learning how to do the things in a particular setting—"learning the ropes"). Dan Duke found many of these same concerns to be present in his analysis (1988) of new principals who were considering leaving the principalship despite the fact that they were generally viewed as being quite effective in their roles. In particular, Duke found that these administrators experienced frustration over the fact that they did not fully understand the nature of leadership responsibilities.

Most studies of beginning administrators have found a consistent set of themes that have implications for the ways in which individuals might be better prepared to take on leadership roles in schools. It seems clear, first, that people should receive a great deal of hands-on learning of administrative tasks and responsibilities before they ever accept their first jobs. Universities, as the agencies traditionally charged with providing preservice preparation for administrators, need to find more ways to help people develop skill and confidence about their work before signing their first administrative contracts. Second, entry-year or induction programs need to emphasize the development of strong norms of collegiality within those who are taking their first administrative jobs, to foster a realization that a school administrator will rarely be effective by trying to "go it alone." A lesson that needs to be learned early in a person's career is that success as a school administrator is often based on the ability to seek support from many people. Third, entry-year programs must include a component that allows people to test some of their fundamental assumptions and beliefs concerning the nature of power, authority, and leadership as they step into a principalship or some other administrative role.

There is not a rich tradition of research into the problems faced by newcomers to the world of school administration. What is known, however, provides some useful insights into the fact that beginners need special assistance and support, and that help should be directed toward consistent themes. Local school systems should draw upon these insights as they determine needs for beginning administrators in their community.

In a project sponsored by the Oregon Society Study Council, Mark Anderson (1988) set out to identify some of the most important themes related to induction programs for school administrators. Anderson developed the following list of recommended practices for school systems that are interested in establishing research-based entry-year programs for administrative personnel:

1. Entry-year programs will be more effective if they are initiated in conjunction with locally developed preservice preparation activities that are carried out for aspiring administrators who are identified in individual school systems.

2. Local school systems that have in place sophisticated techniques designed to identify and select talented future administrators tend to have more effective programs for beginning administrators.

3. Entry-year programs need to include comprehensive activities designed to orient new administrators to the characteristics of particular school systems.

4. Mentor systems designed specifically for the needs of beginning school administrators—not as adaptations of teacher men-

tor programs—are critical components of successful entry-year and induction programs.

5. Effective entry-year programs encourage and facilitate reflective activities. Beginning principals as well as successful veterans are given opportunities to observe each other as a way to reduce newcomer isolation and improve their work through a process of peer support and observation. Such activities need to provide time for reflective analysis between participants.

6. Successful induction efforts are part of more comprehensive districtwide programs designed to encourage professional growth and development for all administrative personnel.

7. Entry-year problems of administrators are minimized in school systems where there has been a conscious effort to structure beginners' workloads so that they would have sufficient time to work in their buildings to develop productive working relationships with staff, students, and parents. School districts should take care not to immerse newly hired principals in a bewildering array of special district projects and committees.

8. Beginning principals have a special need for frequent, specific, and accurate feedback about their performance. This feedback should be of a highly constructive nature and should be made available regularly throughout the school year—not only near the end of a person's first contract year.

These eight ingredients of an effective entry-year program are derived from existing research on this topic. Other sources are available to help guide planners of induction programs by providing some insights into the issue of what should be included in an administrative induction program.

Critical Needs Frameworks

In addition to the general areas of concern for beginning administrators that have been identified through the research, some additional listings of specific critical skills are needed by new leaders. Each of these lists of skills further supports the notion that some kinds of specialized entry-year training activities are needed.

One effort to identify critical skills for beginning school administrators was carried out by the faculty of the Department of Administrative and Educational Leadership at the University of Alabama (1987). The faculty worked with school leaders to identify "survival skills" needed by beginning school administrators. Eight areas of concern were identified, along with several suggested specific competencies in each skill area.

Area I: Leadership
1. Plan and conduct a small-group activity.
2. Write an article about a phase of the school program for publication in the local newspaper.
3. Present a program to the faculty based on "effective schools" research.
4. Develop a faculty handbook.
5. Carry out effective parent–student conferences.
6. Prepare and deliver a speech to a local civic club.
7. Interview prospective teachers.
8. Prepare operational plans for the opening of the school.

Area II: Planning
1. Develop a student master schedule.
2. Apply systematic planning concepts to specific school problems.
3. Develop forms and procedures for reporting unusual incidents that may occur in the school.
4. Develop a proposed calendar for the school year.

Area III: Instruction
1. Develop a plan for evaluating the instructional program of the school.
2. Demonstrate the use of purposeful classroom observation designed to improve instruction.
3. Demonstrate effective classroom management techniques to faculty.
4. Plan and conduct an inservice session for faculty on the proper interpretation and use of standardized achievement tests.

Area IV: Personnel
1. Demonstrate knowledge of certification requirements for teachers.
2. Plan and conduct interviews with teacher applicants.

Area V: Law
1. Demonstrate a knowledge of basic features of procedural due process as it relates to student and staff personnel issues.

2. Demonstrate an understanding of the basic features of the local negotiated agreement between the school board and the teachers' association.
3. Demonstrate knowledge of Public Law (P.L.) 94-142 by explaining regulations to staff.

Area VI: Finance
1. Understand local school accounting procedures.
2. Keep accurate records of building-level accounts.

Area VII: Facilities
1. Develop a plan for energy conservation in the local school building.
2. Develop an emergency evacuation plan for the school.
3. Carry out an inservice session for janitorial and custodial employees.

Area VIII: Community Relations
1. Develop a community relations plan for the local school building.
2. Develop a plan to work effectively with community pressure groups and professional organizations.

Another framework, suggested by Rogus and Drury (1988), might also be looked at by designers of administrator induction programs. They suggest that beginning administrators should be able to:

1. Demonstrate understanding of system expectations, procedures, and resources.
2. Demonstrate increased competence and comfort in addressing building or unit outcomes or concerns.
3. Enhance their personal and professional growth.
4. Develop a personal support program.
5. Receive personalized assistance in coping with unit or building problems.
6. Receive formative feedback and assistance toward strengthening their administrative performance.

Another framework with potential for helping planners of support programs for beginning school administrators was developed by the Maryland Leadership in Educational Administration (LEAD)

Project (1988). Among the skill areas identified in this work were interpersonal relations, instructional supervision, staff development, goal setting, problem analysis, decision making, communication, coordination, conflict management, and stress management.

The frameworks reviewed here represent skills and behaviors beginning administrators need to guarantee success, or at least survival, in organizations. They are what the school needs or expects in terms of performance. Needs have not been discussed from the viewpoint of personal concerns faced by people who serve in administrative roles. There has been much discussion regarding the developmental characteristics of classroom teachers at different points of their careers, and the types of training needs useful in addressing those characteristics. Fuller (1968) and Hall and Loucks (1978) suggested that inservice education should be matched with developmental needs and concerns. A good induction program for administrators must also take into account such varying individual needs as well as organizational priorities.

All these lists of job-related skills include ideas to be used as starting points for the development of the curriculum of an entry-year program. Remembering that local concerns and conditions differ markedly across the nation, a particular school system might have very different expectations regarding the desired performance of new administrators. Before starting an entry-year program, planners should carry out their own research regarding the types of skills, knowledge, and attitudes appropriate for their school system.

Entry-year programs involve more than simply helping people acquire and demonstrate discrete skills that appear on a list. Effective induction programs should be designed in a way that uses identified skill areas as a guide to the development of more expansive programs that address more holistic concerns of beginning administrators. In other words, if entry-year programs become geared exclusively to the development of strategies to be followed in "surviving" the first year of administrative service, a system will be created wherein survivors thrive but do not grow. Instead, a system should be fostered that will continuously develop strong and effective leaders in schools.

Reflections on Needs of Beginning Administrators

Special programs designed to support the work of beginning school administrators are needed. Research shows that novice school leaders will be served well when efforts are made to help them through their first professional duties. But there are limitations to formal induction programs. For example, entry-year programs can never serve to repair total incompetence. School districts need to be careful about finding and selecting only the most talented individuals for administrative roles. No induction program can be designed to correct bad choices.

Entry-year programs must be part of comprehensive professional development efforts. Induction programs for beginning educators will likely fail to reach their full positive potential if they are developed solely as a way to comply with minimal performance expectations. Entry-year efforts will be successful only if they are viewed as a foundation on which school districts set out to build total professional development programs that are designed to meet the needs not only of beginning administrators but of all district administrators.

Summary

An effective entry-year program for beginning school administrators can be built on a solid research base. In this chapter, some of the findings of recent studies that may serve as the foundation for effective induction efforts were offered. In addition, the existence of several alternative frameworks that present locally developed lists of critical needs for novice principals and other administrators were noted.

References

Anderson, Mark. (1988). *Induction programs for beginning principals.* Project Paper of the Oregon School Study Council. Eugene: University of Oregon, College of Education.

Daresh, John C. (1986, Summer). Inservice for beginning principals: The first hurdles are the highest. *Theory into Practice, 25:* 3.

Diederich, Anne Marie. (1988). *Tasks while braiding the tiger's stripes: The transition to the high school principalship.* Unpublished Ph.D. dissertation, The Ohio State University.

Duke, Daniel. (1988). *Transition to leadership: An investigation of the first year principalship.* Portland, OR: Lewis and Clarke University.

Fuller, Frances. (1968). A developmental conceptualization of the concerns of teachers. *American Educational Research Journal, 6:* 178–89.

Hall, Gene E., & Loucks, Susan. (1978, September). Teacher concerns as a basis for facilitating and personalizing staff development. *Teachers College Record, 62:* 81–94.

Marrion, Barbara A. (1983). *A naturalistic study of the experiences of first year elementary school principals.* Unpublished Ph.D dissertation, University of Colorado at Boulder.

Maryland LEAD Center. (1988). *Critical skills for leaders.* Annapolis: Maryland LEAD Center.

Nockels, A. (1981). *The problems, issues, and strategies of the first years of secondary headship.* Report to the Oxfordshire Local Education Authority. Unpublished mimeographed paper.

Rogus, Joseph F., & Drury, William R. (1988). The administrator induction program: Building on experience. *NASSP Bulletin, 72:* 508.

Sussman, Lynne. (1985). *The principal's first year: The mutual process of developing leadership.* Unpublished Ed.D dissertation, Harvard University.

Turner, L. T. (1981). *Preparation for headship.* Unpublished B. Phil. (Ed.) dissertation, University of Birmingham (England).

University of Alabama Department of Administrative and Educational Leadership. (1987). *Survival skills for administrators.* Tuscaloosa: University of Alabama College of Education.

Weindling, Dick, & Earley, Peter. (1987). *Secondary headship: The first years.* Philadelphia: NFER-Nelson.

CHAPTER EIGHT

Induction for What?

In previous chapters, we suggested that a critical component of professional development for school administrators is an approach to providing support during induction. We have promoted the view that a link between preservice preparation activities and ongoing inservice education for administrators is forged through entry-level learning experiences and other forms of personal and professional support.

The belief that beginning educators need some kind of specialized support is not a novel one. At present, at least seventeen states require local school districts to provide induction programs to novice educators (Bowers & Eberhart, 1988; Hawk & Robards, 1987). Recent surveys by the American Association of Teacher Educators (AACTE) (Neuweiler, 1987) and the Illinois State Board of Education (Eastern Illinois University, 1986) have also shown that fourteen states have induction programs for educators in the study, planning, or development stages. These programs have focused on the particular needs of beginning teachers. We have found, however, that the spirit of induction programs for classroom teachers is similar to efforts that may be designed for administrative personnel, even with the restrictions noted in Chapter 6 with regard to placing too much reliance on teacher education concepts when we think about administrator development.

In this chapter, we consider ways of identifying the assumptions and statements of purpose that need to be developed before one actually implements a program for beginning personnel. Unless a school system has a clear understanding of local conditions and of the goals and objectives for induction, such activities may serve as little more than faddish responses to popular national trends. They have little chance of achieving success. We begin by looking at some traditional assumptions that support the adoption of induction pro-

grams for educational personnel. Next, we consider possible purposes that might be addressed through the implementation of structured administrator induction programs. We conclude the chapter
with a consideration of the desired outcome of such efforts: Do we
really want to support school administrators so that they will be
able to serve as school leaders? If that is not the goal, then what
guides our work?

The definition of *induction* that we have selected to guide us is
the one adopted by the Dayton, Ohio, City Schools (1987):

> *Induction is defined as . . . a process for developing among new
> members of an organization the knowledge, skills, attitudes,
> and values essential to carrying out their roles effectively. The
> aim of induction is to create conditions so that the new members
> internalize the norms of their role in a way that the primary
> locus of control is self-control.*

Assumptions of Induction

In 1987 the Association of Teacher Educators (ATE) formed a
special Induction Commission with, as its primary assigned task,
the development of recommendations to be followed by state education agencies, teacher education institutions, and local school systems as they consider the needs of entry-level personnel. The work
of this commission resulted in the following assumptions (Brooks,
1987, p. v):

1. Induction programs are needed in every school district to help
   beginning teachers make a transition from novice to experienced professional.
2. Induction programs must be based on the needs of the individuals as they adjust to their particular professional context.
3. The experienced professionals who serve as sources of help to
   beginning teachers should receive training and support to
   facilitate their assistance, including reduced teaching loads.
4. Support personnel should be concerned with the professional
   development of individual beginning teachers and should be
   separated from the evaluation role of a district.

5. The training of teachers should be recognized as an ongoing educational process from preservice to retirement, requiring cooperative financial and programmatic support from all those involved including the local school district, higher education, and state departments of education.

These assumptions are focused on induction for classroom teachers. We also believe that the fundamental beliefs contained in the ATE list have considerable value for the support of administrative and supervisory personnel beginning their careers. Every school district should have an action plan to address the needs of novice school administrators, although we also recognize that, in smaller systems, new administrators are rare. Second, we endorse the ATE view that induction should be geared to the real needs of individuals in a particular context. Next, we believe that mentors for school administrators—whether at the preservice, induction, or inservice levels of their careers—are so important that they need and deserve special training and support from their local school systems. Fourth, we concur with the view that entry-level support programs should be kept separate from summative evaluation schemes. However, direct feedback in the form of ongoing formative evaluation is a critical component of a good support program for beginners. As a result, we are not wholly supportive of a view that proclaims, in absolute terms, that "induction must *never* involve evaluation, under any circumstance." Beginning administrators are often lost without anyone who is ready, willing, or able to answer the perennial leadership question, "How am I doing?" Finally, we agree with the ATE search for commitment and financial support of a broad-based coalition of agencies when it comes to the design of any induction program.

There is one further assumption that we would like to add to the list that we have reviewed. That assumption is the belief that educational administrators are "worth it." They are worthy of the efforts to create separate induction programs. We believe that the role of the school leader is central to the success or failure of any school and, therefore, to any group of learners. Further, we believe that administration is a distinct form of educational service, related to but apart from the world of daily classroom teaching. As a result, efforts to use too broad a brush to paint the needs of all newcomers to a school system will rarely be successful. Distinctive efforts are needed for each professional role associated with education.

Potential Goals of Induction

Clearly stated goals and objectives are a critical part of an effective administrator induction program. We have identified three possible goals to guide the development of an induction program: remediation, orientation, and socialization. It is crucial that designers of entry-level support efforts decide which of these goals will serve as primary objectives for their work and plan accordingly. No single goal is necessarily more important than the others. However, confusion over the purposes of induction has caused total programs to fail.

Remediation

One of the legitimate objectives of an induction program developed by a local school system is to find ways of remediating some of the earlier training that was (or was not) provided to organizational newcomers. One important goal, then, is to address deficiencies on the part of someone who is first coming on board.

Remediation may seem like a harsh word because it sounds as if the institution that has sent forward the beginner has been at fault, incompetent, or somehow responsible for doing a bad job of getting a person ready for a professional role. Indeed, all of these problems may be present; bad preservice preparation programs, unfortunately, do exist. On the other hand, there are other circumstances that bring about the need for an employing system to remediate new teachers, administrators, or other employees. For example, a person may have gone through an excellent administrator preparation program from a well-respected institution, but that program may not have included coursework in an area such as grant writing or working with severely handicapped student populations. That same person may obtain an initial administrative appointment in a setting where it may occasionally be necessary to write proposals, or to work with low-incidence special needs students. Although these responsibilities might not be so central to a job that great in-depth knowledge would be absolutely essential, it may be important for the successful administrator to understand these issues. As a result, specialized training might be developed to address this deficiency on the part of an individual who is otherwise well qualified to assume a leadership role. This training might be provided by the district as an in-house inservice activity, or the new administrator might be sent to receive specialized training from some external source such as the state department of education, a university, or a professional association.

Another example of how induction serves the goal of remediation is found in the need to provide instruction related to unique local or state policies or practices that may not be known by a person new to an area. An individual who has moved from California, Utah, or New Mexico might be unaware of state regulations and guidelines dealing with certain aspects of budgeting, student record keeping, or teacher grievance and arbitration procedures that might be in force in Colorado or Ohio. It would be understandable for an employing district to address the "deficiencies" of such a beginning school administrator by providing an induction program with a primary focus on remediation.

We believe that it may often be necessary for school systems to address deficits on the part of new administrative personnel. We do not wish to suggest, however, that such efforts can be directed toward making wholly incompetent individuals ready for a job. At times, there are such vast deficiencies on the part of an individual that it may be counterproductive even to attempt to bring that person up to an acceptable level of performance. In short, induction is not a magic recipe; entry-year support programs can never guarantee that people will be successful in their jobs. We are also concerned that employing school districts might hold unrealistic expectations for new administrators or their preservice preparation programs, to the extent that they would believe that no induction for remediation should ever be necessary. In our view, it is not very likely that preservice programs could ever be designed to prepare people to walk comfortably into any administrative role, as if *all* school administrators in *all* school systems *all* across the nation would do *all* the same things. A school system might expect, for example, that all newly hired principals be well versed in the use of Madeline Hunter's approach to the analysis of classroom instruction. However, there are many ways for aspiring administrators to learn about teacher–student interaction, and to assume that, if a person is not fully conversant in Madeline Hunter, then the preservice program (and the candidate) are to be blamed, is incorrect. There will always be a need to "fix" newly hired personnel to some extent, regardless of the quality of preservice training. But the extent to which such remediation is necessary must be tempered by some clear awareness of skills that might be reasonably expected of all newcomers.

Orientation

Another objective for induction programs is to provide new-comers with information concerning local policies, practices, and procedures. This type of learning experience is normally described as new employee orientation. Here, people learn about such issues as how to request materials or services from various divisions within the school system (e.g., "Where do I go to get a broken desk in my school fixed?"), to whom one should go for additional information about a topic of interest (e.g., "Who will tell me about social service agencies that are available for some of the students in my school?"), and the nature of policies that relate to daily administrative concerns (e.g., "What am I supposed to do with vendor contracts for services and materials in my school?"). Induction programs related to basic orientation typically include information dealing with traditional employee concerns such as health and dental insurance packages, retirement benefits, tax deduction options, and so forth.

Orientation for newly hired administrators is important, but we also have a few concerns about these efforts. First, when orientation programs are provided in a perfunctory, cut-and-dried fashion, they offer little for newcomers to learn about issues that are personal concerns. Not all principals might need to know about health maintenance plans in precisely the same way as all other principals. Not every new administrator has a burning desire to know about optional retirement plans that will be available after thirty years of service. Some school systems equate induction programs completely with employee orientation. When we propose that all school districts devote time and other resources to assist new administrators, we mean that there is a need to do considerably more than bring the new principals over to the central office one afternoon in August to receive copies of the school board policy manual and talk to someone from the personnel division about benefits packages.

Socialization

The third goal of a structured induction program concerns the issue of providing a form of socialization, defined by Theodorson and Theodorson (1979, p. 396) as the process "through which an individual becomes integrated into a social group by learning the group's culture and his role in the group." Daniel Duke (1987) noted that there are three distinct forms: anticipatory, professional, and organizational socialization. All of these processes are designed to help the organizational newcomer find an answer to the question, "What's going on around here?" However, there is a specialized meaning to each of these three perspectives.

Anticipatory socialization is defined as the "learning of the rights, obligations, expectations, and outlook of a social role preparatory to assuming it" (Theodorson & Theodorson, 1979, p. 397). Duke (1987) and Blumberg and Greenfield (1980) noted that this form of socialization occurs throughout much of the life of future administrators before they actually accept a first job. As classroom teachers, and even earlier, as students in school, future administrators learn about their chosen craft by observing the role of the school administrator from afar. As Duke noted, "By the time people actually assume positions of school leadership, they are likely to have learned a great deal about how to act and what to expect as school leaders" (1987, p. 262).

Duke (1988, p. 22) noted that *professional socialization* for school principals "encompasses learning about the field of administration and how administrators, as opposed to non-administrators, make sense of the world." According to Duke (1988, p. 22), examples of activities that make up professional socialization include the following:

— Acquiring schoolwide, as opposed to classroom-based, perspectives on matters of curriculum, instruction, evaluation, and resource allocation
— Understanding the ways in which the effectiveness of administrators, teachers, and schools can be judged
— Learning the ethics and laws governing administrative behavior
— Recognizing areas where professional norms may conflict with organizational norms

Organizational socialization may be described as the process by which new administrators learn to function in a particular organizational (school and district) context (Duke, 1988, p. 22). This form of socialization is addressed not through orientation programs but, rather, through a much more complex and subtle process wherein newcomers are expected to learn about norms and the culture of the new school setting. Among the specific ingredients are the following (Duke, 1988, p. 23):

— Learning the expectations for principals and the criteria by which the district evaluates them
— Understanding how experienced principals have functioned in the district
— Understanding the district's goals
— Understanding the nature of the community and the school in which the principal will work
— Learning survival skills, such as how to turn off the fire alarm and how to fill out purchase orders
— Reviewing organizational history—local policies, regulations, guidelines, and why they were developed

Organizational socialization represents a way of becoming aware of the nuances of organizational life not always addressed in simple descriptions of institutional rules, regulations, and procedures.

Of the three types of socialization detailed here, only professional socialization and organizational socialization might be addressed directly as parts of formal induction programs. We doubt that any strategy can be developed to address the concept of anticipatory socialization. Rather, we believe that such a concept might best be addressed as part of preservice preparation.

Is Leadership the Goal?

We return to the question that serves as the title of this chapter. Toward what goal are we directing efforts to provide induction for beginning school administrators? There are two possible paths that might be followed by those who design such programs.

The first path is toward basic survivorship, or helping newcomers survive their first years on the job. Activities might be directed toward helping people to make it through a first job experience. Although we recognize the importance of helping people to survive a potentially rocky start in their careers, we are also concerned that the development of induction solely to promote survivorship might be misplaced energy. Accepting the view that induction should be directed only at helping people to survive a first year on the job is not effective for two reasons. First, induction is not a one-year commitment of support. Moving into a new professional role is often an activity that may take two or three years to accomplish, particularly when one considers the complexity of such things as professional and occupational socialization. Second, an emphasis on survivorship suggests a minimalist approach to professional development. If the goal is only to survive, no further growth may occur.

A second path might lead to the search for long-term leadership skills. In this regard, induction is a long-term commitment to excellence and professional development. We support this vision because it suggests that induction programs are designed in a way that might use identified skill areas as a guide to the development of more expansive programs that address the holistic concerns of beginning administrators. If induction programs become exclusively geared to the development of programs and strategies that are to be followed in "surviving" the first year of administrative service, a system will be created in which survivors thrive. Instead, a system should be fostered that will develop strong and effective leaders in schools.

Summary

In this chapter, we considered some objectives that might be pursued through the development of local induction programs for school administrators. First, we considered some of the traditional assumptions for induction programs developed for beginning educators. We noted that the majority of the recent literature in this area has focused on the needs of beginning classroom teachers. We indicated that many of the basic assumptions related to teachers might also apply to school administrators. Next, we reviewed three goals of structured induction programs: remediation, orientation, and socialization. With regard to the third issue, we distinguished among three types of socialization: anticipatory, professional, and organizational socialization. The latter two are within the purview of induction programs, whereas anticipatory socialization is mostly a function of preservice preparation. Finally, we considered the issue of whether administrator induction should be directed toward the promotion of survivorship or leadership. In our view, leadership development is the only legitimate goal for an induction program.

References

Blumberg, Arthur, & Greenfield, William. (1980). *The effective principal.* Boston: Allyn and Bacon.

Bowers, G. Robert, & Eberhart, Nancy. (1988, Summer). Mentoring for first year teachers in Ohio. *Theory into Practice, 27,* 4:38–51.

Brooks, Douglas M. (Ed.). (1987). *Teacher induction: A new beginning.* Papers from the National Commission on the Induction Process. Reston, VA: Association of Teacher Educators.

Dayton (Ohio) City Schools. (1987). *Entry year program for administrators.* Dayton, OH: Board of Education.

Duke, Daniel L. (1987). *School leadership and instructional improvement.* New York: Random House.

Duke, Daniel L. (1988). *Thoughts on the preparation of principals.* Unpublished paper, University of Virginia.

Eastern Illinois University. (1986). *Final report of the initial year of teaching study.* Chicago: Illinois State Board of Education.

Hawk, P. P., & Robards, S. (1987). Statewide teacher induction programs. In D. M. Brooks, (Ed.), *Teacher induction: A new beginning.* Reston, VA: Association of Teacher Educators.

Neuweiler, H. B. (1987). *Teacher education policy in the states: Fifty state survey of legislative and administrative actions.* Washington, DC: American Association of Colleges for Teacher Education.

Theodorson, George A., & Theodorson, Achilles G. (1979). *A modern dictionary of sociology.* New York: Barnes and Noble.

CHAPTER NINE

Mentoring for Beginning Administrators

As educational reformers have come up with different ways to improve schooling practices, two strategies have been suggested. During the 1970s and early 1980s, the primary thrust of effective schools research was directed toward identifying factors found in schools with high-quality student achievement scores. Berliner and Tikunoff (1976) carried out studies to determine the effectiveness of in-classroom activities, while Edmonds (1979) and Mortimer (1988) identified characteristics of effective schools beyond teacher–student interactions. More recently, efforts to find more effective schools have led to suggestions for reforming the preservice preparation and induction of school personnel. Current research strives to find effectiveness by focusing on institutions traditionally charged with the responsibility for preparing teachers and administrators.

In this chapter, we explore the use of *mentoring* as a way in which newcomers to professional education roles are made ready for their responsibilities. Our focus here is on the ways in which mentoring supports the induction of beginning school administrators. We begin by providing a general overview of mentoring, with emphasis on its application in settings both within and outside of the field of professional education. Next, we take a look at the value that mentoring has for addressing the needs and concerns of beginning administrators. Third, we consider some of the practical issues associated with the design and implementation of mentoring programs for school leaders. We conclude the chapter by outlining the things that might be included in a program designed to prepare experienced school administrators to serve as mentors to beginning colleagues.

Existing Literature on Mentoring

In this section, a review of recent literature describing mentoring is provided. First, several basic definitions are considered. Next, the use of mentoring relationships outside the field of education is described. Third, some of the ways in which the concept of mentoring has been applied within professional education are examined.

Definitions of Mentoring

In recent years, mentoring relationships have been extremely popular, and their application has been viewed as a panacea for dealing with many of the limitations often felt to exist in education as well as in many other fields.

Using mentoring relationships to enhance professional development activities is not a new idea. The concept of the mentor serving as a sort of wise guide to a younger protege dates back to Homer's *Odyssey*. Mentor was the teacher entrusted by Odysseus to tutor his son, Telemachus. On the basis of this literary description, we have been provided with a lasting image of the wise and patient counselor serving to guide and shape the lives of younger, less experienced colleagues.

This image of mentoring persists in many of the most recent definitions of this practice. Ashburn, Mann, and Purdue (1987) defined *mentoring* as "the establishment of a personal relationship for the purpose of professional instruction and guidance." Lester (1981) noted that this activity is an important part of adult learning because of its holistic and individualized approach to learning in an experiential fashion, defined by Bova and Phillips (1984) as "learning resulting from or associated with experience."

Other related definitions are found. Sheehy (1976) defined a mentor as "one who takes an active interest in the career development of another person . . . a non-parental role model who actively provides guidance, support, and opportunities for the protege. . . ." The Woodlands Group (1980) called mentors guides "who support a person's dreams and help put [the dream] into effect in the world. . . ." Levinson (1978), in his analysis of the socialization of young men to professional roles, noted that a mentor, as a critical actor in the developmental process, is

> *one defined not in terms of the formal role, but in terms of the character of the relationship and the function it serves . . . a*

mixture of parent and peer. A mentor may act as host and guide welcoming the initiate into a new occupational and social world, and acquainting the protege with its values, customs, resources, and cast of characters.

Another definition, by Wasden and his associates, (1988) is directly related to mentoring for educational administrators:

The mentor is a master at providing opportunities for the growth of others, by identifying situations and events which contribute knowledge and experience to the life of the steward. Opportunities are not happenstance; they must be thoughtfully designed and organized into logical sequence. Sometimes hazards are attached to opportunity. The mentor takes great pains to help the steward recognize and negotiate dangerous situations. In doing all this, the mentor has an opportunity for growth through service, which is the highest form of leadership.

The element that serves as the foundation of any conceptualization of mentoring is the fact that this activity must be a part of the true developmental relationship that is tied directly to an appreciation of life and career stages. Kathy Kram (1985) examined mentoring in private industry and observed that different types of relationships are appropriate at various times in a person's career. She divided these times into early, middle, and late career years and suggested that people tend to have vastly different mentoring needs in each of these time frames. "Research on adult development (Levinson, 1978; Gould, 1978) and career development (Hall, 1976; Schein, 1976) has established that, at each stage of life and a career, individuals face a predictable set of needs and concerns which are characteristic of their particular age and career history" (Kram, 1985, p. 37). In education, "mentors" usually retain the same titles and responsibilities without regard for the different needs and interests of people who need mentoring. The only recognition of varying support is found in the recent emphasis on mentoring for first-year teachers now found in at least sixteen states (Bowers & Eberhart, 1988).

Embedded within this notion of the mentor serving as a guide to adult development is the expectation that this person is to engage in the mid-life task of generativity, or "concern for and interest in guiding the next generation" (Merriam, 1983). This practice includes "everything that is generated from generation to generation:

children, products, ideas, and works of art" (Evans, 1967). This function of mentoring is a form of "torch passing" from one generation to the next.

There are also some potentially harmful consequences of mentoring. For example, mentoring can be detrimental to growth if and when proteges develop too great a reliance on mentors, who are expected to provide all possible answers to all possible questions. In such cases mentoring no longer exists; rather, a type of dependency relationship is formed, and growth by the protege is rarely possible.

Most current definitions place great emphasis on the ways in which the mentor provides support and guidance to the protege. However, such one-way relationships are not the only characteristics of mentoring. In fact, this relationship might also be described as a mutually enhancing one (Kram, 1985), whereby the career advancement and personal development of each participating member is addressed. This view emphasizes that mentoring may be as beneficial to the mentor as it is to the protege.

Mentoring is described as an accepted and vital part of the developmental processes in many professional fields. As Schein (1978) noted, the concept has long been used in business organizations to connote such diverse images as "teacher, coach, trainer, positive role model, developer of talent, opener of doors, protector, sponsor, or successful leader." The literature suggests that mentoring needs to be understood as a combination of most, if not all, of these individual role descriptors (Galvez-Hjornevik, 1986). Thus, mentoring must be included in any experiential professional development program. Guides, counselors, or coaches (if the term *mentor* becomes overused) are needed to help neophytes negotiate their way through a field and make sense out of what is happening around them in an organization, and also what is going on in their personal lives. As a result, there is considerable potential to be found in applying the concept of mentoring to the professional development of school administrators (Daresh, 1988).

Mentors are different from the role models who work with aspiring or beginning administrators in conventional field-based learning activities. Kram (1985) noted that other terms that might be used to describe developmental relationships in work settings include "sponsorship," "coaching," "role modeling," "counseling," and even "friendship." Shapiro, Haseltine, and Rowe (1978) suggested that there is a continuum of advisory relationships that facilitate access to positions of leadership in organizations. At one extreme is a "peer pal" relationship, and at the other end of the continuum is the true mentor relationship:

Peer pal: Someone at the same level as yourself, with whom you share information, strategies, and mutual support for mutual benefit

Guide: Someone who can explain the system but is usually not in a position to champion a protege

Sponsor: Someone less powerful than a patron in promoting and shaping the career of a protege

Patron: An influential person who uses his or her own power to help a protege advance in his or her career

Mentor: An intensive paternalistic relationship in which an individual assumes the role of both teacher and advocate.

The developmental relationships described here are business oriented in that they are designed primarily to foster career advancement and development. Similar perspectives are offered by many others, including Dalton, Thompson, and Price (1977), Anderson and Devanne (1981), Van Vorst (1980), and Clutterbuck (1985).

Mentoring Outside Education

The current literature incorrectly makes it appear that the concept of mentoring was only recently invented by professional educators. Mentoring has long been recognized as an important activity in the world of private business and industry. Here, younger members of the organization are shown the ropes and led toward greater success through the intervention of others who provide the direction necessary to achieve personal goals and ambitions. The example of senior colleagues is a key to finding greater happiness and fulfillment on the job. This type of mentor–protege relationship has been an informal one, where both parties tend to gravitate toward one another on the basis of such things as common goals, interests, and other factors that cannot be arranged by others. A senior staff member sees promise in "the new kid," takes an interest in that person's professional life, and, over time, provides feedback to the younger co-worker so that he or she will have a better chance to succeed in the organization. The value of this type of mentoring is seen by many companies as an activity that deserves to be institutionalized, encouraged, and even required as a standard practice for all new employees. Keele, Buckner, and Bushnell (1987), among others, have noted that formal, organizationally sponsored and endorsed mentor programs have been initiated in settings such as the Internal Revenue Service and many large commercial banks and insurance companies. In these and other situations where mentoring has been viewed as an effective strategy that may serve to promote personal and professional development, the bringing of new leaders "on board" assumes many of the following characteristics noted by Henry (1987):

1. Mentoring arrangements are a small but important part of normal management training for selected employees.
2. What is typically referred to as *mentoring* often tends to be, in fact, an activity of "coaching," or showing people "how we do it around here."
3. Organizational cultures support the development of future managers, and thus there are typically certain formal or informal rewards associated with mentoring as well as being mentored.

Private industries have recognized for quite some time that informal mentor–protege relationships exist, and that these pay dividends to the organization as well as to the individuals involved. As a result, they are viewed as having sufficient value to warrant the creation of more formalized, institutionally created and supported mentoring arrangements.

Another area where the concept of mentoring has received considerable attention in recent years has been the identification and development of leadership skills by women moving into executive roles (Bolton, 1980; Shakeshaft, 1987). One great barrier to women seeking advancement to mangerial positions has historically been the lack of other women available to serve as role models and mentors in superordinate positions in many organizations. There are few women who are in positions higher up in the system, who can open doors to individuals ready to assume greater authority, responsibility, prestige, or power. As a result, the mentor has been seen as a person who is essential to helping the individual woman learn how to cope with the realities of a system by pointing out the proper routes to follow, the situations to avoid, and the ways to behave if she wishes to become more successful in the workplace (Daloz, 1983). The mentor–protege relationship for women going into management (or any other professional role, for that matter) tends to be an informal, natural, and evolved one that is typically not structured and created by the employing system. It is a type of mentoring that simply "happens."

Mentoring in Professional Education

Within the past few years, the potential value of mentoring as a feature of professional development for educational personnel has been appreciated and understood more completely (Krupp, 1985; Krupp, 1987; Zimpher & Reiger, 1988). It is now generally accepted that wise, mature mentors have always been around to help new teachers learn their craft in ways that were not usually covered in most preservice teacher education programs at the university level (Gehrke & Fay, 1984; Gehrke, 1988). What is now taking place with considerable regularity and visibility, particularly in the area of teacher education, is the development of formal, contrived, and institutionally supported mentoring programs. Studies by Krupp (1985), Little, Gallagher, and O'Neal (1984), Showers (1984), and Huling-Austin, Barnes, and Smith (1985) have described the importance of mentoring relationships as a way of helping classroom teachers become more effective, and have suggested that mentoring programs must be deliberately started as a way to enhance the quality of induction for teachers new to classrooms. Eagan and Walter (1982) studied a group of elementary school teachers early in their careers and found that those individuals who had mentors credited them with helping the proteges to gain self-confidence, learn technical aspects of their jobs, understand the expectations of administrators, develop creativity, and work effectively with others. These and many other studies of the value of mentoring for teachers (Hardcastle, 1988) have led at least seventeen states (Bowers & Eberhart, 1988) to mandate mentoring systems for beginning teachers.

Potential of Mentoring for Beginning Administrators

The job of the mentor appears to be one that will continue to play a significant role in future schemes designed to improve the quality of educational personnel in general, with special attention now being paid to school administrators. As emphasis has been placed on efforts to find strategies for preparing school leaders that go beyond traditional university-based programs, there is a corresponding awareness that mentoring is an important concept that has implications for the ways in which beginning and aspiring administrators might enjoy more successful transitions from the world of teaching to the world of administering.

Mentoring has at least two potential applications to improve the ways in which people become school administrators. The first of these is related to the identification of individuals who would serve as appropriate role models for beginning administrators. Frequently the term *mentor* is assigned to the experienced administrator who happens to be available to answer the questions of novice colleagues. It would be desirable for such individuals to become true mentors to the beginning administrators with whom they work, and such a relationship may evolve. Being a sponsor, patron, or role model, however, is by no means the same thing as being a true mentor in the ways beginning administrators need as part of their initial professional formation. It is crucial for someone to work with the new administrator to describe procedures, policies, and normal practices in a school or district. It is also critical that someone be able to provide feedback to beginners concerning the extent to which they have been able to master the technical skills associated with the performance of administrative roles.

A second potential value of the concept of mentoring as part of a program for the induction of beginning administrators is found in its application to formation. Mentoring is an absolutely essential part of this dimension, whether at the preservice, induction, or inservice phase of professional development for school administrators.

In the induction of beginning school administrators, there are distinct differences between the duties of a role model and those of a mentor. A role model may be seen as a person who is consulted periodically by the novice as a way to learn how to construct a master schedule for a school, observe a teacher, conduct a student–parent conference, or perform many other daily activities, in much the same way that an apprentice may learn practical skills from a master tradesman. On the other hand, a mentor goes beyond this modeling function by serving as a person who is inclined to prod the beginner to learn how to do something according to his or her personal skills and talents. In short, mentors are likely to raise more questions than provide answers to the people with whom they interact.

Mentoring as part of the professional development of beginning school administrators is a critical responsibility. Consequently, a person who would serve as a mentor must possess the deep desire to act in this capacity. An ideal arrangement for mentoring would involve the careful matching of proteges with ideal mentors. There would be a one-to-one matching based on analyses of professional goals, interpersonal styles, learning needs, and perhaps many other variables that might be explored prior to placing beginning administrators with their mentors. In the real world of schools, it is nearly impossible to engage in such perfect matching practices. Most mentoring relationships that are formed to comply with the expectations of the state guidelines for the induction of school administrators will be formed as "marriages of convenience," and not as ideal, naturally developed partnerships. Still, we believe that an awareness of the potential values of mentoring, as well as a review of some of the basic issues to be addressd in conceptualizing such programs, will be helpful to those who are expected to provide leadership to entry-year programs for school administrators.

Practical Issues in Mentoring Programs

The development of effective mentoring programs involves a great deal of attention to many specific issues prior to the first efforts at the implementation of such activities. In this section, the characteristics of good mentors and some problems and issues that need to be faced as part of the design of any comprehensive program are addressed.

Characteristics of Mentors

A number of desired characteristics are listed here to aid in the selection of mentors for administrative entry-year programs (Daresh & Playko, 1990):

1. Mentors should have experience as practicing school administrators, and they should be generally regarded by their peers and others as being effective.
2. Mentors must demonstrate generally accepted positive leadership qualities, such as (but not necessarily limited to):

   a. Good (oral and written) communication skills
   b. Intelligence
   c. Past, present, and future understanding with simultaneous orientation

d. Acceptance of multiple alternative solutions to complex problems

e. Clarity of vision and the ability to share that vision with others in the organization

f. Well-developed interpersonal skills and sensitivities

3. Mentors need to be able to ask the right questions of beginning administrators, and not just provide the "right" answers all the time.

4. Mentors must accept "another way of doing things," and avoid the temptation and tendency to tell beginners that the way to do something is "the way I used to do it."

5. Mentors should express the desire to see people go beyond their present levels of performance, even if it might mean that they are able to do some things better than the mentors themselves can do the same things.

6. Mentors need to model the principles of continuous learning and reflection.

7. Mentors must exhibit an awareness of the political and social realities of life in at least one school system; they must know the "real way" that things get done.

In addition, Patricia Haensly and Elaine Edlind (1986) suggest the following characteristics of "ideal" mentors:

1. Outstanding knowledge, skills, and expertise in a particular domain

2. Enthusiasm that is sincere, convincing, and, most important, constantly conveyed to their proteges

3. The ability to communicate to others a clear picture of their personal attitudes, values, and ethical standards

4. The ability to communicate sensitively the type of feedback that is needed regarding the protege's development and progress toward desirable standards of competence and professional behavior

5. The ability to listen sensitively to their protege's ideas, doubts, concerns, and enthusiastic outpourings

6. A caring attitude and a belief in their protege's potential

7. Flexibility and a sense of humor

8. A restrained sense of guidance so that their proteges may develop as independently as possible

There are also some characteristics of individuals that signal that they might not be effective as mentors:

1. Ineffective mentors are those who are too heavily involved with the internal politics of a school system, to the extent that their primary goal is to survive the system and increase their personal status within the district. It is important for a newcomer to understand the political realities of a school system, but it is not important for a new person to learn how to spend most of his or her time simply jockeying for position.

2. It is not typically a wise move to arrange a mentoring relationship between a novice and a person who is also new to his or her position as a mentor. This is true even if the mentor has many years of experience at another position in the system. For example, a former experienced principal in his or her first year in a central office position frequently has so many things to learn that he or she may need a mentor, and may not have the time to spend with a beginning principal.

3. Mentors should not be assigned because the school system believes that such an assignment will serve to "fix" a marginally effective administrator. Although it is true that service as a mentor has been shown to be a way to increase the mentor's effectiveness, it does not make good sense to match a beginner with anyone who is not able to demonstrate the very best behaviors associated with being an educational administrator.

4. Ineffective mentors have a long history of high staff turnover rates in their buildings or in their school districts.

5. Ineffective mentors demonstrate know-it-all behaviors and attitudes when discussing their approaches to dealing with administrative problems. Clearly, self-confidence is a desirable characteristic for a mentor. Being closed-minded about alternative solutions to complex problems, however, is probably a mark of a person's insecurity and lack of confidence. Such features would not qualify a person as a particularly effective mentor.

The use of mentoring is widely supported as a valuable approach to professional development for people in many different fields. However, there are some problems:

1. Mentors may become too protective and controlling.
2. Mentors may have personal agendas to fulfill, at the expense of proteges.

3. Beginning principals may get only a limited perspective from a single mentor.
4. Mentors may not acknowledge the limitations of their proteges.
5. Beginners may become too dependent on their mentors.
6. Beginners may idolize and idealize their mentors.
7. Beginners may try to become carbon copies of their mentors.
8. Formal mentoring arrangements may be too structured.
9. Mentors may try to hold all beginning principals to an ideal vision or standard of performance which may never be realized.

Responsibilities of Mentors

Despite any apparent limitations on the use of mentoring as a central part of induction programs for school administrators, tremendous value may be achieved through these programs. Most benefits are achieved when mentors become engaged in carrying out a variety of special functions and responsibilities:

1. *Advising:* In this way, the mentor responds to a protege's need to gain additional information needed to carry out a job effectively.
2. *Communicating:* Here, the mentor works consistently to ensure that open lines of communication always exist between himself or herself and the protege.
3. *Counseling:* The mentor provides needed emotional support to the protege.
4. *Guiding:* The mentor works to orient and acquaint the new administrator with the formal and informal norms of a particular school system.
5. *Modeling:* The mentor serves as a true role model to the protege by consistently demonstrating professional and competent performance on the job.
6. *Protecting:* When needed, the mentor serves as a buffer between the protege and those in the school system who might wish to detract from the beginner's performance.
7. *Skill development:* The mentor assists the protege in learning skills needed to carry out the job effectively.

In addition to these listed responsibilities, the mentor must also be willing to provide the time that a beginning administrator may need simply to talk about job-related concerns. Perhaps the most important thing that anyone can do as a mentor is to be available when needed by the protege, not to "fix" problems but, rather, to indicate that someone cares about the beginner.

Benefits of Mentoring

There are many benefits to be derived from a well-designed mentoring program. These benefits might best be described in terms of things that are likely to assist the person serving as a mentor. Clutterbuck (1985) identified three major sets of benefits to be derived by those who serve as mentors: improved job satisfaction, increased peer recognition, and potential career advancement.

The greatest number of rewards for mentors are found in the area of improved job satisfaction. Here, mentors find that grooming a promising new administrator is a challenging and stimulating personal experience, particularly if the mentor has reached a point in his or her own career where a lot of the earlier excitement is disappearing. Mentors often find that their service in this capacity is rewarding in other ways. One example of this is found when proteges are successful and perform their jobs well. Mentors also report a sense of satisfaction in seeing the values and culture of a school system handed over to a new generation.

Mentors indicate that the mentoring experience is worth it because they get increased recognition from their peers. In private business, a mentor who identifies a promising employee often acquires a reputation for having the type of insight into the needs of the company that should be rewarded. Such a benefit is not likely to occur in educational administration mentoring programs designed to support beginners. However, it is likely that some mentors have in the past and will continue in the future to identify and tap talented teachers and other staff members in their schools to go into school administration.

Finally, mentors also indicate that they find satisfaction in their role because it often gives them opportunities for personal career advancement. In this regard, a major payoff is found in the way mentors benefit from the energy and enthusiasm of their proteges. The mentor receives new ideas and perspectives by allowing proteges to add their own insights into the ways in which organizational problems are addressed. Mentors who are attentive to the potential of those with whom they interact are able to capitalize on a new source of knowledge, insight, and talent, and they may be able to translate this into their own professional growth and advancement. Indeed, wise "old dogs" may learn many "new tricks" from some "young pups," if they are wise enough to stop and listen.

Mentor–Protege Matching

Matching mentors with proteges is neither an easy nor a precise task. It would be highly desirable to match every beginning administrator with a mentor who possesses a sincere and deep desire to spend time working productively with a novice. Such commitment may not always be available, however, particularly in very small school systems where few administrators are available to serve as mentors.

The ideal matching of mentors and proteges should be based on an analysis of the professional goals, interpersonal styles, and learning needs of both parties. It is often nearly impossible to engage in such perfect matching. However, if individual awareness of the values to be found in mentoring, a regard for mutual respect and trust, and a sense of openness and positive interaction are all present, then the mentor–protege relationship has the greatest potential to be a strong one.

No magic recipes exist to guide the matching of mentors with proteges, but some of the issues that might be considered when a school district begins to develop a local program include the following:

1. Cross-gender mentoring (Will it be possible for men to work effectively with female colleagues? For women to work with men?)
2. Mentoring across organizational levels (Can a superintendent serve as a mentor to a beginning principal?)
3. Differences in ages (Can younger, but more experienced, administrators serve as effective mentors to older colleagues who are just beginning their administrative careers?)
4. Mentoring across school systems (Is it necessary for the mentor and protege to be employed by the same school system? Can

productive mentoring relationships be developed across school district boundaries?)

Answers to all of these questions must be addressed at the local level because of the specific conditions that persist in different settings. Further, local conditions such as the personalities of administrators, traditions of cooperation, and other aspects of life in a particular system have a major impact on the way in which a program might be developed.

Specialized Training for Administrative Mentors

School districts that are about to implement administrator induction programs will likely find it necessary to develop specialized training activities to help those individuals who have been identified as mentors to carry out their responsibilities as effectively as possible.

Four conditions need to exist if mentor training is to be effective. A system undertaking the establishment of a mentoring program will take steps to establish trust and openness among the administrators of the district, to invest sufficient resources to support a mentoring program, to develop and maintain open and honest communication patterns, and to show awareness and sensitivity to the unique learning needs of adults.

A model may be reviewed as a possible outline to be followed by a local school system that would like to develop an intensive approach to preparing individuals to serve as administrative mentors. In order to develop, formulate, and implement a program like this, certain procedures must be followed to ensure the general success of the program and its acceptance by district personnel. This process is cyclical in nature, and each step provides incremental development and acceptance of the program. There are ten generic steps that are useful in the implementation of a mentoring program:

1. Getting a commitment from the district central administration and school board
2. Establishing a board policy
3. Developing a planning team that will coordinate the efforts of the program at the local district level
4. Assessing needs that should be evaluated through the program

5. Planning a budget
6. Allocating human and material resources needed for the program
7. Designing the structure
8. Developing appropriate goals and objectives for the program
9. Implementing the program
10. Evaluating the program

Once initial planning has taken place, and after the selection of mentors has been carried out, the actual training may be implemented. This should be based on what has already been identified through existing literature as important learning for mentors. The training model that we suggest contains six domains that we believe reflect the realities of administrative life as well as preparing individuals to become effective mentors for beginning administrators (Daresh & Playko, 1989). These domains are (1) appreciation of a validated knowledge base, (2) instructional skills, (3) mentoring skills, (4) human relations skills, (5) district needs, and (6) personal formation. This model is designed to provide a foundation in the development and refinement of an independent, effective, successful, instructional leader. Each domain is equal and all are interdependent.

Appreciation of a Validated Knowledge Base

Often, an individual will make decisions based on the preferences and demands of the crowd, or on personal biases. It would be helpful to develop an orientation for proteges to seek validated information before making decisions. This would occur if individuals were actively involved in contributing to the development of research in the profession, or actively using research as a way to inform practice. Principals should be aware of their school environment, the needs of individuals within their schools, and the nature of trends and practices that would be appropriate and best serve the needs of those individuals.

Instructional Leadership Skills

The key ingredient in effective schools is the principal. If this person has the ability to serve as an instructional leader, then the school will become more effective as student learning is enhanced.

At least part of the time involved in a program designed to train administrative mentors must involve a review of the specific skills associated with instructional leadership.

Mentoring Skills

Training must devote time to reinforcing the view that the mentor and protege are both participants in the mentoring "team." In order for the relationship to be a positive one, the mentor needs to be available to offer assistance, support, and guidance to the beginning principal. This availability could be to observe the protege in action and then share some insights derived from this process. Training must focus on the development and promotion of peer-to-peer relationships.

Mentors need training to help them realize that this is a major commitment of time, effort, and energy. It should be a valuable experience, shared by the mentor and the protege alike. Realizing that there are peaks and valleys built into any intense working relationship is important, and part of the mentor training must be directed toward this understanding.

Human Relations Skills

Mentoring is based on a mutually enhancing relationship. It is important for the mentor to be knowledgable about the psychological and humanistic aspects of relationships in order to create successful communication skills and listening skills, and to cultivate other abilities such as honesty, trustfulness, sincerity, and sensitivity. In addition, part of the training experience should be devoted to increasing mentors' awareness of adult learning needs.

School District Needs

This domain involves the review of issues and concerns that are unique to the individual school district in which the mentor–protege programs are to be implemented. Time must be provided as part of the training exercise to address the issue of "who, when, what, and how" things get done in particular districts. Mentors need to receive general orientations to the goals of their districts, important policies, and procedures that are particularly important in each district. In this way, proteges will learn about committees, personnel, and the general structure of the organization in which they will work.

Personal Formation

The final domain is related to helping mentors work with their proteges in the area of personal formation. A major responsibility of a mentor must be to help his or her protege understand personal abilities while assuming a new professional role.

Training may be provided in a number of important concepts. Perhaps the most important of these involves the development of reflective processes. Incorporating reflective actions into one's behavioral repertoire is important.

Summary

In this chapter, the use of mentoring was presented as it relates to support systems for beginning school administrators. Such an activity has the potential to serve as a central feature of structured induction programs. It was also noted that mentoring is not easy to achieve and that it should not be viewed as a panacea for all the problems that novice school leaders may encounter.

A number of issues were considered. First, a review of related literature was presented. Next, the specific application of mentoring to support programs for beginning school administrators was considered. Third, a number of the practical issues associated with mentoring programs were examined, including such things as the ideal characteristics of effective mentors, and how mentors may be matched with proteges. The chapter concluded with a number of suggestions for activities and concepts that should be included in training programs that are used to prepare individuals to serve the important role of mentors to beginning school administrators.

References

Anderson, C., & Devanne, M. (1981). Mentors: Can they help women get ahead? *Career Development Activities, 2,* 2:5–8.

Ashburn, E. A., Mann, M., & Purdue, P. A. (1987). *Teacher mentoring: ERIC Clearinghouse on Teacher Education.* Paper presented at the annual meeting of the American Educational Research Association, Washington, D.C.

Berliner, David, & Tikunoff, William J. (1976). The California Beginning Teacher Evaluation Study: Overview of the ethnographic study. *Journal of Teacher Education, 27:*24–30.

Bolton, B. (1980). A conceptual analysis of the mentor relationship in the career development of women. *Adult Evaluation, 30:*195–207.

Bova, B. M., & Phillips, R. R. (1984). Mentoring as a learning experience for adults. *Journal of Teacher Education. 35,* 3:196–210.

Bowers, G. Robert, & Eberhart, Nancy A. (1988, Summer). Mentors and the entry year program. *Theory into Practice. 27,* 3:226–230.

Clutterbuck, R. (1985). *Everybody needs a mentor.* London: Institute Press.

Daloz, L. (1983). Mentors: Teachers who make a difference. *Change, 15,* 6:24–27.

Dalton, G. W., Thompson, P., & Price, R. L. (1977). The four stages of professional careers: A new look at performance by professionals. *Career Dynamics, 6:* 19–42.

Daresh, John C. (1988, April). *The role of mentors in preparing future principals.* Paper presented at the Annual Meeting of the American Educational Research Association, New Orleans, LA.

Daresh, John C., & Playko, Marsha A. (1989). *Administrative mentoring: A training manual.* Greeley: University of Northern Colorado Center for Educational Leadership.

Daresh, John C., & Playko, Marsha A. (1990, September). Characteristics of administrative mentors for principal development. *NASSP Bulletin.*

Eagan, M. M., & Walter, G. (1982). Mentoring among teachers. *Journal of Educational Research, 76:* 113–118.

Edmonds, Ronald (1979, October). Effective schools for the urban poor. *Educational Leadership. 37,* 1:15–24.

Evans, R. (1967). *Dialogue with Erik Erikson.* New York: Harper & Row.

Galvez-Hjornevik, C. (1986, January–February). Mentoring among teachers: A review of the literature. *Journal of Teacher Education, 37,* 1:6–11.

Gehrke, Natalie, J. (1988, Summer). Toward a definition of mentoring. *Theory into Practice, 27,* 3:190–194.

Gehrke, Natalie, J., & Fay, R. S. (1984). The socialization of beginning teachers through mentor-protege relationships. *Journal of Teacher Education, 35,* 3:21–24.

Gould, R. (1978). *Transformations: Growth and change in adult life.* New York: Simon and Schuster.

Haensly, Patricia A., & Edlind, Elaine P. (1986). *A search for ideal types in mentorship.* Paper presented at the First International Conference on Mentoring, Vancouver, British Columbia.

Hall, D. T. (1976). *Careers and organizations.* Pacific Palisades, CA: Goodyear.

Hardcastle, Beverly. (1988, Summer). Spiritual connections: Proteges' reflections on significant mentorships. *Theory into Practice, 27,* 3:201–208.

Henry, J. E. (1987). *Internships and mentor programs.* Paper presented at the annual meeting of the American Educational Research Association, Washington, D.C.

Huling-Austin, L., Barnes, S., & Smith, J. (1985). *A research-based development program for beginning teachers.* Paper presented at the annual meeting of the American Educational Research Association, Chicago.

Keele, R. L., Buckner, K., & Bushnell, S. J. (1987). Formal mentoring programs are no panacea. *Sloan Management Review, 22,* 5:67–68.

Kram, Kathy E. (1985). *Mentoring at work: Developmental relationships in organizational life.* Glenview, IL: Scott, Foresman.

Krupp, Judy-Arin. (1985). *Mentor and protege perceptions of mentoring relationships in an elementary and secondary school in Connecticut.* Paper presented at the annual meeting of the American Educational Research·Association, New Orleans, LA.

Krupp, Judy-Arin. (1987). Mentoring: A means of sparking school personnel. *Journal of Counseling and Development, 64:* 154–155.

Lester, V. (1981). The learning dialogue: Mentoring. *Education for Student Development.* New Directions for Student Services, No. 15. San Francisco: Jossey-Bass.

Levinson, Daniel. (1978). *Seasons of a man's life.* New York: Knopf.

Little, Judith W., Gallagher, P., & O'Neal, R. (1984). *Professional development roles and relationships: Principles and skills of "advising."* Contract No. 400-83-003. San Francisco: National Institute of Education.

Merriam, Sharon. (1983). Mentors and proteges: A critical review of the literature. *Adult Education Quarterly, 33,* 3:161–173.

Mortimore, P. (1988). *School matters: The junior years.* London: Open Books.

Schein, Edgar. (1976). *Career dynamics: Matching individual and organizational needs.* Reading, MA: Addison-Wesley.

Shakeshaft, Carol. (1987). *Women in educational administration.* Beverly Hills, CA: Sage.

Shapiro, E. C., Haseltine, F., & Rowe, M. (1978). Moving up: Role models, mentors, and the patron system. *Sloan Management Review, 19:* 51–58.

Sheehy, Gail. (1976, August 12). The mentor connection: The secret link in the successful woman's life. *New York Magazine,* pp. 33–39.

Showers, Beverly. (1984). *Peer coaching and its effects on transfer of training.* Paper presented at the annual meeting of the American Educational Research Association, Chicago.

Van Vorst, J. R. (1980). *Mentors and proteges among hospital chief executive officers in Indiana.* Unpublished Ph.D. dissertation, Indiana University.

Wasden, Del F. (1988). *The mentoring handbook.* Provo, UT: Brigham Young University.

Woodlands Group, The. (1980). Management development roles: Coach, sponsor, and mentor. *Personnel Journal, 24,* 6:57–61.

Zimpher, Nancy, & Reiger, Susan R. (1988, Summer). Mentoring teachers; What are the issues? *Theory into Practice, 27,* 3:175–182.

CHAPTER TEN

Research on Administrator Inservice

An important feature of effective schools is the quality of the leadership demonstrated by individual school building administrators. Good schools have good principals. Although a great deal of attention has been paid to the importance of the school administrator as a key to educational improvement, little systematic study has been made of the inservice education needs of school leaders. We assume that leadership in schools is important, but we know relatively little about how leadership can be supported and made stronger. In addition, current conditions found in American education dictate the need for educators to be aware of emerging trends and practices in the field of inservice education. Providing for professional growth opportunities for those who work in schools will be a priority for many years to come. Special attention is reserved for and deserved by those who serve in formal leadership roles.

In this chapter, we express the view that we need to design more effective programs for administrator inservice education. As a way to help build that foundation, we devote this chapter to an overview of the status of recent research related to the inservice education of practicing school administrators. We will address three questions:

1. How has administrator inservice typically been studied in the past?
2. Toward what objectives has past research been directed?
3. In what directions might future research proceed?

In the sections that follow, we consider possible answers to each of these three major questions. We assume that a review of studies of past inservice practices may serve us well in our efforts to construct more effective planned learning experiences for administrators in the future.

How Has Administrator Inservice Been Studied?

We recently completed an analysis of original research on inservice education for school administrators in the United States (Daresh, 1985). Over a ten-year period, nearly fifty studies were conducted of the ways in which educational administrators are provided with learning opportunities while on the job. One of the factors that prompted us to look at this work was a desire to determine how ongoing inservice education for practicing school administrators has been studied. We looked at the data collection procedures used in the studies and also at the specific educational roles that were examined.

Research Designs

The most frequently employed research design for studies of administrator inservice was the descriptive survey. Twenty-eight of the studies reviewed were of this type. The next largest groups were quasi-experimental and "action research"—seven studies of each type. There were no longitudinal, historical, or true experimental studies, and only three case studies and two correlational studies were included.

Data Collection Procedures

Most studies made use of only one data collection technique and in most cases that technique was the researcher-designed questionnaire. Interviews were used in about 20 percent of the studies, and document analysis or direct observations were used approximately 10 percent of the time. More than one data collection procedure was used in only about one-quarter of the studies.

Roles Studied

Studies looked either at school administrators in general (i.e., central office and building-level administrators), or at specific positions (i.e., the principalship or the superintendency). Twenty-six studied general administration, and the remainder examined particular roles. Of this latter group, seventeen studies focused on the principalship.

Overview of Methodology

After reviewing methods used in research on inservice education for practicing school administrators, we conclude the following:

1. Inservice education and professional development for classroom teachers have been well studied in recent years. Inservice education for school administrators has been investigated much less thoroughly.

2. Widely disseminated professional education journals contain few reports of original research related to administrator inservice.

3. The relatively few studies of inservice education for school administrators have had a problem-solving (rather than a theory-testing or theory-building) orientation, and most of them have been descriptive surveys that made heavy use of questionnaires as the sole data collection device. Absent from the scene are analyses that view inservice education as part of a broader vision of professional development for aspiring as well as practicing educational administrators. In addition, little evidence is found of studies that give much attention to theoretically grounded issues such as adult learning and development.

4. The administrative role that has attracted the greatest amount of attention by recent researchers has been the principalship, with nearly equal attention being paid to elementary and secondary school administrators. Central office administrators, as a broad classification, receive the second greatest amount of attention. Virtually no studies can be located that deal solely with the role of the superintendent of schools and with inservice education needs.

Toward What Objectives Has Recent Research Been Directed?

Completed research falls into one of the following broad categories: (1) content of inservice; (2) procedures used in the delivery of inservice; (3) the effects of inservice programs on teachers, administrators, or others; or (4) the development, evaluation, and validation of inservice education programs and modules for practicing school administrators. It is not always easy to classify studies because they often fall into more than one of those categories. Nevertheless, we can make some generalizations that should be of use to those who are either planning future studies, developing new programs, or refining existing practices.

Content of Inservice

Twenty-one of the studies that were reviewed dealt either exclusively or in part with inservice participants' preferred training topics and content of inservice education. Findings across these studies were:

1. Administrator inservice education is viewed as more effective when content is based on the needs of the participants.

2. Desired administrator inservice education content tends to be concerned with topics of immediate concern to participating practitioners. Nancy Pitner's finding in her analysis of administrator inservice training (1983) is still accurate: The first choice of practitioners still appears to be programs related to effective time management—no matter how much time it takes! Other examples of this finding are evidenced in the number of programs that deal with "how to" implement programs mandated by local school systems, state departments of education, or as a consequence of federal guidelines. Less interest was expressed in issues related to the development of more effective human relations skills, and almost no interest was shown toward inservice education designed to increase administrators' conceptual skills.

3. There appeared to be few relationships between specific selected background characteristics of school administrators and desired inservice education content. There was a finding that a moderate correlation existed between the age and years of administrative experience of individuals and their preferred inservice education topics. Younger and less experienced administrators placed much greater emphasis on the acquisition of concrete technical skills that they believed were needed to carry out the daily responsibilities of performing their jobs.

Procedures for the Delivery of Inservice

Sixteen studies examined the preferred methods to be used in the planning and carrying out of effective administrator inservice education. Some of the generalizations that could be made were:

1. Administrators want to be involved in the planning of inservice, including the selection of learning activities and objectives.

2. Administrators prefer inservice education activities that make use of active participant involvement rather than one-way communication techniques such as lectures. Administrators do not wish to go to sessions where they feel that they are being "talked at." Interestingly enough, the use of such "preaching" formats is cited frequently by classroom teachers as a primary source of frustration when they, in turn, deal with school administrators.

3. Inservice education training activities are viewed as much more effective when they are part of a coherent staff development program that continues over an extended period of time. One-shot ("dog-and-pony show") sessions that promise simple solutions to complex organizational problems are not seen as particularly realistic or useful. This appears to be somewhat of a contradiction, however, from the first generalized finding that suggested that administrators are enamored with quick, "how-to-do-it" types of sessions.

4. As participants in inservice education learning activities, school administrators want to decide the goals, delivery techniques, evaluation procedures, and other aspects of the design of the training.

Effects on Teachers and Administrators

Eleven studies investigated the effects of inservice education training activities on either teachers or administrators. No one has looked into the issue of whether administrator inservice has any discernible effects on students, school board members (and their perceptions of administrator effectiveness), or any other individuals who might be expected to notice changes in administrative effectiveness. The only generalized finding that came from these studies was that administrator inservice has no apparent impact on the attitudes of teachers or administrators. Only one study reported that there had been a significant impact on the knowledge level of administrators after receiving training on procedures associated with the implementation of P.L. 94-142.

No information was found concerning the long-term and follow-up effects of administrator inservice. It was simply an issue ignored in the research literature. One might assume that this is the result of the lack of longitudinal studies, a factor largely due to the high percentage of doctoral dissertations that made up the studies that were reviewed. For rather obvious reasons, doctoral students simply do not engage in longitudinal research.

Model Development and Evaluation

Fourteen studies were directed toward the development of a local model of inservice education for practicing administrators, along with the subsequent evaluation and validation of that model. In these studies, the primary concern of the researcher was the validation of the model and not the impact of the inservice training per se, although impact on administrators' or teachers' knowledge, skills, or attitudes generally served as the dependent variable. Most of these studies made use of a quasi-experimental design wherein the treatment group was asked to respond to some type of pretest instrument and then was given some type of training. The overall experience was then validated through the administration of some type of posttest questionnaire. When change occurred in the treatment group, the inservice program was presumed to be effective. All but one of the fourteen studies that followed this pattern found that the locally developed inservice experience was successful. Although there are some flaws in this work, the intriguing part of most of these studies is that there appears to be an almost universal absence of additional research using the same local inservice model in a variety of other settings. As a result, it is virtually impossible to obtain much corraborative evidence regarding the effectiveness of inservice education training programs developed for school administrators.

Future Directions

After reviewing the status of research on administrator inservice training in terms of predominant research designs and methodology, and also according to the major purposes cited for the research, a few summary statements are possible. Changes are called for in many aspects of the present situation with respect to research on inservice education for practicing school administrators.

Changes in Research Methodology

Too much reliance has been placed on only one type of research design, the descriptive survey. The few quasi-experimental studies that have been conducted have been directed almost exclusively toward the validation of local inservice education models, and the "action research" has been of only limited value regarding its ability to increase our knowledge of the overall field. Investigations that are classified as action research appeared to be little more than narrative descriptions of localized inservice programs. As a result, Hopkins's (1983) view that action research should probably more properly be called a form of curriculum development, and not research at all, seems warranted.

The minimal presence of case studies is not only perplexing, but of considerable concern as well. Given the amount of research and suggested emphasis recently placed on this approach to research in recent years, and also based on its apparent suitability for the analysis of administrative processes and behaviors (Bridges, 1982), this is quite surprising. The absence of true longitudinal studies in education is due to the large number of investigations carried out by doctoral students, who rarely want to prolong their academic programs by continuing to collect data over an extended period of time. But this absence serves to limit our knowledge concerning the possible long-term effects of administrator inservice on the knowledge, attitudes, and skills demonstrated by practitioners.

There is nothing inherently wrong with well-designed survey research. Our concern here, however, is that many other forms of research could also be used to improve our overall understanding of inservice education for school administrators.

Changes in Data Collection Procedures

Research on administrator inservice education is certainly not unique in its frequent use of the questionnaire as the primary (if not sole) data collection device. Any review of the procedures used in the majority of educational studies will reveal that data for most studies are gathered through the administration of a research-designed instrument that is meant to be used in only one particular study. It would be desirable to see some changes made in the ways in which researchers collect information about inservice education programs for school administrators. For example, there is a surprising absence of on-site, naturalistic research techniques employed to determine what really goes on during the course of "typical" inservice training sessions. It is unfortunate that interview studies of administrators regarding their inservice education expectations and preferences are not found in any great numbers. In general, ethnographic data collection methods are noticeably lacking in this field.

Knowledge production about administrator inservice is also limited by what seems to be an overdependence on research instruments that are designed for use in only one study at a time. Besides the obvious questions related to the validity and reliability of these types of data-gathering devices, we also wonder whether the use of such constantly changing measures will lead us to the creation of a knowledge base, or even to reinforcement of the belief that research on administrator inservice education must necessarily be a case of only finding out more and more about less and less.

Changes in Research Orientation

Most studies of administrator inservice education have been directed toward problem-solving goals and have not been related to any identified theory base in the social sciences. Of the forty-seven studies reviewed, only three were clearly based on any discernible theory, and all three made use of constructs derived from established theories of organizational change. Before there can be a meaningful development of inservice practice, efforts must be made to develop a richer conceptual description of this field. This description might well be based on what we think we already know about such domains as decision theory, leadership theory, or social systems theory. Such a search for stronger conceptual footing might involve a shift away from approaches to research that are almost exclusively directed at solving problems in the here and now, and toward investigations that might challenge much wider assumptions about the nature of effective inservice, adult learning, and administrative development in general. The field of educational administration was considerably enriched by the "theory movement" of the 1950s and 1960s, which permitted the study of administration to move beyond the reactions to one problem after another to a considerably more analytical level, which allowed generalizations concerning the role and function of educational organizations and their leaders.

Changes in Roles Studied

Perhaps the one area of existing research related to inservice education for practicing school administrators that needs little modification deals with the selection of administrative roles to be studied. There is overwhelming support in the literature for the importance of the role of the building principal as the key promoter of effective schools, and the review of research related to administrator inservice shows clearly that the principalship indeed receives more attention than any other role. The only observation we make here is that future researchers should not ignore other administrative positions in their studies. We have much to learn about many specific educational roles, and the time may come when there is, in fact, an overabundance of interest in the principal's role, and a virtual absence of any serious attention paid to the superintendent or other central office administrators.

Changes in Research Objectives

There is no real need to modify the stated purpose of research directed toward administrator inservice. There should be a pronounced emphasis on inservice content, how that content is actually delivered and presented, and whether the presentation of that content is perceived as effective and has had an impact on the existing knowlege, skills, or attitudes of administrators. What we will need in the future, rather, is more detailed information about each of these areas. It is not enough, for example, to continue to learn time and again that administrators want to be involved with the selection of training activities and specific learning objectives. We already have ample evidence from studies of adult learning, staff development, and inservice education for teachers to suggest that people like to be involved in training design. What we have little information about at present are the specific conditions that are related to that general finding. We do not know if there are times when people would actually prefer to have little or no involvement in selecting training activities or objectives. This is only one example of the type of greater detail that researchers may need to explore in the future if we are ever to develop a substantial knowledge base related to administrator inservice.

Summary

The changes reviewed here are just a few that could be made regarding the ways in which we study inservice education for practicing school administrators. There are other important issues that need to be considered as well. For example, do reserachers have a clear understanding of the general goals and objectives of professional development for school administrators? Is inservice education merely a way for administrators to keep abreast of the latest technical information that they need to do their present jobs on a day-to-day basis? Or are there some larger goals, as we have suggested throughout this book, that ought to drive programs of professional development? Are there some techniques and strategies for inservice design that appear to be absolutely ineffective? If so, why do these seem to persist?

In this chapter, we suggested that learning about administrator inservice is quite important. We make that statement because of a strong assumption that we have made throughout this book, namely that the ultimate goal of administrator professional development must be the enhancement of activities designed to bring about educational improvement. If school administrators are going to fulfill the leadership functions that have been assigned to them, researchers must be willing to examine quite seriously the ways in which leadership can be enhanced and supported.

References

Bridges, Edward M. (1982). Research on the school administrator: The state of the art. *Educational Administration Quarterly, 18,* 3: 12–33.

Daresh, John C. (1986). Status of research on administrator inservice. *National Forum of Educational Administration and Supervision, 3,* 1: 23–31.

Hopkins, C. P. (1983). *Understanding educational research.* Columbus: Merrill.

Pitner, Nancy J. (1983). Training of the school administrator: State of the art. (Occasional Paper). Eugene, OR: Center for Educational Policy and Management, University of Oregon.

CHAPTER ELEVEN

Traditional Model of Inservice

The first of the alternative models for the delivery of ongoing inservice education for practicing school administrators is the traditional model. This is perhaps the most frequently employed strategy, and it consists of school administrators enrolling in university courses for graduate credit.

In this chapter, we review the characteristics of this traditional strategy for providing continuing learning experiences for practicing school administrators. We begin by reviewing some of the characteristics of effective inservice education that have been identified in recent literature in this field. This serves to guide our analysis of the traditional and other models of inservice delivery included in the next few chapters. Next, we examine the structural characteristics of the traditional model as a way of clarifying what we mean by this particular strategy. Third, we look into some of the most often cited advantages or positive features of this model. We conclude this chapter with an exploration of some of the major disadvantages of the traditional approach to using university courses as a way to deliver administrator inservice.

Effective Inservice Practices

Hutson (1981) described the status of research on inservice education as "deplorable" because hard research is meager, and broad-based conceptualizations are lacking. Despite this situation, enough has been produced to enable a number of reviewers (Lawrence, 1974; Nicholson, 1976; Paul, 1977; McLaughlin & Marsh, 1978;

Hutson, 1981) to extract generalizable propositions regarding the planning and implementation of effective inservice education:

1. Effective inservice education is directed toward local school needs.
2. Inservice participants need to be involved in the planning, implementation, and evaluation of programs.
3. Effective inservice is based on participant needs.
4. Adult learning processes, rather than passive techniques such as lectures, are viewed as desirable and effective inservice instructional methods.
5. Inservice that is part of a long-term, systematic staff development plan is more effective than a one-shot, short-term program.
6. Local school inservice must be backed up by commitment of time, money, and other material resources from the central office.
7. Effective inservice provides evidence of quality control and is delivered by competent presenters.
8. Programs that enable participants to share ideas and give assistance to one another are viewed as successful.
9. Inservice programs are effective when they are designed so that individual participants' needs, interests, and concerns are addressed.
10. Rewards and incentives, both intrinsic and extrinsic, must be evident to program participants.
11. Inservice education activities should be provided during school time.
12. Effective inservice education requires ongoing evaluation.

As noted earlier, little research related to administrator inservice is available to guide our efforts beyond these twelve generalizations. As we proceed through our review of a variety of generic administrator inservice models in the next few chapters, we will refer to these propositions to guide us in understanding some of the strengths and weaknesses of each model.

Structural Features of the Traditional Model

The traditional model of administrator inservice consists of making use of existing university graduate-level courses as a way to enhance the professional development learning opportunities of practicing school administrators. Thus, when one considers the nature of this inservice model, one also considers the structure of the majority of instructional practices available in most universities across the nation.

The primary responsibility for determining the content and specific delivery methods for instruction in this inservice model lies with the university. More precisely, content and instructional methodology are selected by the individual faculty members who teach certain courses. Principals and other administrators select the traditional model as a delivery system based on a desire to pursue additional formal coursework in an area of professional interest, to obtain an advanced graduate degree, to renew or upgrade administrative certification or licensure, or some combination of all of these purposes.

The traditional model of administrator inservice is a highly institutionally defined type of learning experience. It is not designed to serve as a learning activity with an immediate payoff for a particular individual or group of partcipants. It is not the normal goal of a professor of educational finance to share some tips of the trade that will help a local superintendent to find ways to pay for creative curriculum redesign efforts.

Advantages of the Traditional Model

There are a number of advantages associated with the traditional university course as a model for the delivery of administrator inservice. One of the greatest of these is the fact that this approach relies heavily on the existing university structure, a structure that more often than not assures that some degree of quality control has been exercised on a learning experience. Grades, course syllabi, and regular class schedules provide the type of framework in which principals and others who enroll in the courses are able to know essentially what they will get in return for their investment of time, hard work, and money. Also, the content of most university courses is generally the product of at least some advance planning concerning a given topic by a qualified professional educator. Cynics might note here that such "advance planning" is little more than periodic review of twenty years of teaching, which relies on the same old yellowed lecture notes. Conceptually, however, most university courses do not represent attempts to provide a "quick fix" for the sorts of complex problems faced so often by school practitioners.

Disadvantages of the Traditional Model

There are also some weaknesses in the use of the traditional university courses as a form of administrator inservice education. Perhaps the greatest of these resides in the university's attempt to provide relevant learning experiences to practitioners out in the field. There is something contradictory in the expectation that one agency, such as an institution of higher education, would endeavor to meet the organizational needs of another institution, namely public schools. Regardless of the needs of practitioners, "the self interest of the university prevails in terms of the usual offering of courses" (La-Plant, 1979, p. 3). This is coupled with the recognition that the quality of inservice is directly related to the quality of the institution that is providing instruction. Another shortcoming is that the individual administrator who is enrolled in a university course is only a passive participant in the learning process. One-way communication from professor to student prevails in most university classes, and there is typically little or no involvement of participants (i.e., students enrolled in the classes) in selecting course goals, objectives, and activities. The traditional model is also limited because motivation to participate is generally external to the participant; the administrator is most often pressed to take a course by some type of mandate from an external group such as the state education agency or the university. Finally, the use of university courses for ongoing administrator inservice typically lacks power because courses are most frequently designed to serve an entirely different cleintele; they are meant to be taken by those who aspire to some professional role, not by individuals who are already out in the "real world." The lack of leveling of courses is a particular problem in universities that lack the size or resources to allow the development of special topics courses, seminars, or other learning experiences that might expand curricular offerings.

We examine the traditional model in light of the characteristics of effective inservice practice listed earlier in this chapter. University courses represent a form of systematized and ongoing learning that is not greatly affected by short-term trends or fads. Second, university courses are normally delivered by individuals who possess some degree of expertise related to the material being presented, even if these individuals may not always possess great entertainment skills or, perhaps, the degree of expertise that they imagine they do! Most universities also attempt to guarantee at least a minimal amount of quality control over the courses they offer. Finally, the university structure is one that tends to call for ongoing evaluation of programs and courses. Although some might question whether or not the results of university course evaluations are really consulted, it is common practice for institutions to expect that professors will engage in course evaluations each term.

The university course tends to fare poorly when it is examined according to some of the other criteria for determining effective inservice education practices. For example, the typical course is not particularly sensitive to individual participants' needs or to the conditions that exist in some local school systems. Then again, university courses would probably lose some of their potency as experiences designed to change individuals and organizations if they were too "user-friendly." In short, university courses are excellent ways for participants to earn degrees, satisfy scholarly curiosity, or meet state certification requirements. As long-term solutions to the need for more effective forms of administrator inservice education, however, they are quite limited. In our recent analysis of principals' perceptions of the quality of different administrator inservice models (Daresh, 1988), we found that administrators frequently participate in university courses, but they do not rate these learning experiences as particularly effective.

Summary

In this chapter, we looked at the use of graduate-level university courses as one way to provide ongoing inservice education to practicing school administrators. We referred to this strategy as the traditional model of administrator inservice.

We began by listing twelve characteristics of effective inservice education that have been identified in the literature and may serve as a screen to be used in the assessment of any approach to inservice. Next, we provided a brief overview of the structural components of the traditional model and noted that most individuals are aware of the nature of this approach because it is the standard university course taken so often by so many. We completed our analysis of the traditional model by noting a number of advantages and disadvantages often associated with this form of learning.

References

Daresh, John C. (1988, April). *An assessment of alternative models for the delivery of principal inservice.* Paper presented at the annual meeting of the American Educational Research Association, New Orleans.

Hutson, H. M. (1981). Inservice best practices: The learnings of general education. *Journal of Research and Development in Education, 14:* 1–10.

LaPlant, James C. (1979). *Inservice education for principals.* Dayton, OH: Charles F. Kettering Foundation.

Lawrence, Gordon. (1974). *Patterns of effective inservice education.* Tallahassee: Florida Department of Education.

McLaughlin, M. P., & Marsh, D. D. (1978). Staff development and school change. *Teachers College Record, 80:* 69–94.

Nicholson, A. M. (1976). *The literature on inservice teacher education: An analytic review.* Inservice Teacher Education Project Report No. 3. Washington, DC: U.S. Office of Education.

Paul, Douglas. (1977). Change processes at the elementary, secondary, and post-secondary levels. In J. Culbertson & N. Nash (Eds.), *Linking processes in educational improvement.* Columbus, OH: University Council for Educational Administration.

CHAPTER TWELVE

Institutes

The most popular inservice strategy available to practicing school administrators is the *institute*. A variety of other terms might be used to describe this strategy, including the short-term workshop or seminar. The duration of these learning experiences also varies. Some workshops last only a few hours or a single day. Professional conferences and conventions may last as long as several days or even weeks. All of these activities fit within our definition of the institute as an inservice education model.

The institute is any type of relatively short-term learning activity that is directed toward a single specific topic or a narrow range of related topics. This approach is distinct from the other inservice education delivery models because the institute is a short-duration activity, and it tends to deal with such highly focused special topics that it might be more properly referred to as an isolated training event rather than ongoing inservice programming. Still, the pervasiveness of the institute is such that it cannot be ignored in this overall treatment of alternative learning experiences available to school administrators.

Institutes are readily available inservice learning activities. Practitioners are offered a wide array of programs by a multitude of sponsoring agencies and sources. The typical sponsors of most institutes are state, regional, or national professional associations for school administrators, state departments of education, and colleges and universities. In addition to the instructional values and objectives of institutes, sponsoring them is appealing because they represent significant opportunities for producing revenues. As a result, individual private entrepreneurs have increasingly entered the business of providing structured inservice programs in the form of institutes for educational administrators.

Advantages of Institutes

Institutes have a number of positive features. First, their structure makes it possible for a good deal of information concerning issues of immediate concern to be presented to practitioners. As examples, consider the number of recent workshops that have popped up on topics such as restructuring schools, special education, the use of microcomputers for school management, AIDS education, substance abuse detection, prevention, and treatment, site-based managment techniques, and teacher evaluation. Related to this is the fact that institutes can generally be designed quickly to serve the immediate needs of busy practitioners whenever issues and concerns warrant some sort of specialized training. With laws, policies, and technologies changing rapidly, flexibility in training is a highly prized feature of any approach to inservice education. Another strength of this model is that institutes are convenient learning activities. Given the number of offers for workshops, seminars, and other similar training events that flood the mailboxes of practicing administrators, it would be hard to imagine that anyone would have much trouble finding a relevant or interesting training event. Clearly, then, there is strength to be found in the extent to which this approach to inservice can provide for immediate relevance.

Disadvantages of Institutes

The disadvantages of institutes are similar to some of their advantages. For example, the short duration of training events usually means that they are convenient, but it also means that no great depth of treatment on topics—often very complex topics—can be expected by institute participants. At best, institute participants receive only limited treatment of important issues. Not much time can be given for reading, preparation, and assimilation of material during the few days—or hours—that are devoted to the training. This is no problem if the content of the training is such that it can be adequately understood in a relatively short period of time. When issues addressed are more complex, however, time limitations may force these issues to be made trivial. Another drawback is that short-term training events lack opportunities for participants to become involved in setting training objectives, determining content, and selecting specific learning activities. Also, communication patterns in most institutes tend to be one-way, from institute speakers and staff to participants. In a study of participants' perceptions of the relative effectiveness of a number of administrative inservice models, Daresh (1988) found that institutes were the most readily available and utilized approach to inservice education. However, they were rated quite low in terms of their ability to promote effective patterns of ongoing dialogue and professional learning among participating school administrators.

A final drawback to the application of institutes is that quality control may be a concern. Although the majority of institutes that are sponsored by professional associations for school administrators, state education agencies, and universities are perceived as effective by most participants, caution is necessary in the case of some of the advertised experiences. Short-term training events can quickly degenerate into ineffective, though slick, "dog-and-pony shows." Claims are often made that the information learned in one brief weekend session will somehow serve as a quick solution to highly complex problems, which most will recognize as issues requiring a considerably greater long-term commitment. In one recent case, a high-powered team of consultants offered to spend two full days on site in any school system in the country to develop an "absolutely foolproof approach to dealing with the dismissal of incompetent teachers." We have no idea whether or not any school administrators attended these sessions. We suspect, however, that no perfect solutions were offered. Snake oil salesmen, in the mold of the nineteenth century medicine show doctors, are still very much alive and well and with us.

We understand why busy school leaders are tempted to look for quick and easy ways of dealing with the multitude of complex problems they face in their jobs. However, it is never likely that easy responses will be available with no investment of time or talent.

Examples of Institutes

Although institutes as a form of inservice learning are sponsored by a wide variety of agencies, the groups that have the greatest experience with the promotion of this form of activity are the professional associations that include large numbers of practicing school administrators. The National Association of Secondary School Principals (NASSP), the Association for Supervision and Curriculum Development (ASCD), Phi Delta Kappa (PDK), the National Association of

Elementary School Administrators (NAESP), the National Middle Schools Association (NMSA), and the American Association of School Administrators' (AASA) National Academy of School Executives, as well as the efforts of local and state affiliates of these groups, are prime examples of professional associations' efforts to provide inservice opportunities via the institute model. Similar training events are also sponsored by state education agencies, universities, private foundations, and individual consultants.

As a way to illustrate the types of issues that are often addressed through institutes sponsored by professional associations, we turn our attention to the offerings of at least two groups, the NASSP and the ASCD. Both of these sponsoring agencies have long-standing positive reputations for providing high-quality learning experiences for professional educators. Further, both associations rely on the institute model as a source of considerable revenue to sustain the other activities of their organizations.

National Association of Secondary School Principals

As its name implies, this organization, with approximately 16,000 active members, strives to provide professional assistance to practicing administrators who are involved with education in high schools, junior high schools, and middle schools across the United States and Canada. The NASSP makes a full range of services available to its members, including the sponsorship of numerous student activities such as the National Honor Society, life and liability insurance packages, legal advice, and a number of publications such as the *Newsleader* and the widely read practitioner journal, the *NASSP Bulletin*. Another way in which the association addresses the needs and interests of its members is through the sponsorship of many different institutes throughout each school year.

There are two major strands of institutes promoted by the NASSP each year. The first consists of the national convention, an event that normally attracts 5,000 to 6,000 people for a four-day meeting in mid-year to such attractive locations as Orlando, San Diego, Anaheim, or New Orleans. The programs for these conventions include many opportunities for job-alike gatherings of administrators from middle, junior, or senior high schools; for rural and small-school principals; and for principals from urban school systems. There are also numerous presentations by nationally recognized speakers representing not only the educational community, but also such fields as sports, the media, politics, or private industry. Small-group discussion sessions also take place during the term of the convention, and topics discussed during these meetings tend to focus on the sharing of information concerning effective practices used by administrators who experience common problems faced by many of their colleagues across the nation.

The second strand of short-term learning events sponsored by the NASSP includes short-term sessions that are designed to provide practicing secondary school administrators with up-to-date information on topics and issues that are of immediate relevance to any school administrator interested in doing an effective job.

Institutes are offered at desirable locations during the year, with warm-weather sites being particularly well advertised during the winter months. There is no question that, in addition to their role as highly accessible learning activities for many school administators, there is some wisdom in offering these activities as opportunities for vacations as well. It is crucial for organizations such as NASSP to adopt such a policy because considerable organizational operating funds are typically generated each year by inservice activities that are made available to member administrators.

Association for Supervision and Curriculum Development

The Association for Supervision and Curriculum Development (ASCD) includes some 17,000 members, primarily in the United States and Canada. Unlike the NASSP, this association includes a wide array of different role incumbents within its membership. Administrators, classroom teachers, supervisors, directors of specialized educational programs and services, state department officials, and university professors all belong to the ASCD.

The association has both a national and a regional focus. Each state has its own local ASCD organization. In addition, the ASCD provides inservice opportunities for its members through four different sources. First, it provides an extensive selection of published material, including the widely read journal *Educational Leadership*. The association also produces a large number of other written materials each year, such as briefing papers on curriculum trends and an annual yearbook, which includes a large number of thematic chapters developed by highly respected scholars and practitioners in a number of areas of specialization within the broad areas of curriculum and supervision.

The association also provides members and others interested in the field of educational leadership a number of opportunities for learning about new developments and effective practices in such areas as staff development, curriculum development and evaluation, and instruction. This is accomplished through an annual convention, which, like the annual meetings of many national organizations, tends to be held in attractive, warm-weather settings during the winter months, and regional inservice institutes that are offered around the country throughout the year.

The annual ASCD convention features a fairly typical array of sessions wherein papers are presented concerning topics of interest to practitioners and others. Most ASCD national meetings, however, also have two very different features. For one thing, this group tends to attract participation from a rather wide array of different constituent groups. It is not unusual to find school administrators, classroom teachers, state department officials, and university professors attending the same sessions. Thus, ASCD meetings are unlike meetings of the American Educational Research Association, for example, where the majority of participants are professors, and unlike those of the American Association of School Administrators, where most convention attendees are central office administrators and school board members. Second, the ASCD always provides for in-depth treatment of complex educational issues as part of its annual meetings. Each year a portion of the annual meeting agenda is devoted to "action labs" where individuals devote an extended period of time to issues such as mastery learning, thinking skills, or clinical supervision practices.

The other form of ongoing inservice education sponsored by the ASCD is the regional curriculum institute, where a large array of topics are made available to association members and other educators each year. These institutes are offered throughout the United States. As a result, a deliberate effort is made to provide for the convenience of those with an interest in a particular issue.

Summary

In this chapter, we reviewed yet another generic model used in the delivery of inservice education for school administrators, the institute. We also noted that some might refer to this model as a short-term seminar or even as a workshop.

We noted that this model is readily available to most practicing school leaders. Professional associations, state departments of education, universities, and private entrepreneurs all provide institutes for those with a particular interest. We also noted that this availability is one of the greatest strengths of this model. Indeed, there is rarely a question of whether or not one can find a workshop. Rather, the more appropriate question appears to be whether or not one can choose the correct learning experience.

Among the shortcomings of institutes, it is often difficult to ensure that these approaches to inservice are always high-quality programs led by individuals who are truly competent.

We concluded the chapter by reviewing the institute offerings of two national associations, the National Association of Secondary School Principals and the Assocation for Supervision and Curriculum Development. We noted that these two groups have been consistent in their offering of high-quality programs to practicing school leaders for many years.

Reference

Daresh, John C. (1988, April). *An assessment of alternative models for the delivery of principal inservice.* Paper presented at the annual meeting of the American Educational Research Association, New Orleans, Louisiana.

CHAPTER THIRTEEN

Inservice Academies

Many school districts and other educational agencies have created their own forms of inservice education made available to practitioners—teachers, administrators, and all other educational personnel—on an ongoing basis. In this chapter, we will explore these locally developed programs as we describe another generic model for the delivery of inservice education for school administrators, the *academy*.

We begin by defining more precisely what we mean by inservice education academies. Next, we look at some of the advantages and disadvantages associated with this inservice model. We complete our review of the academy by providing a few brief descriptions of how this model has been implemented in a few settings across the nation.

Structure of the Academy

The inservice education academy is an arrangement wherein a school district, a state department of education, or some other educational agency provides structured learning experiences to educators on an ongoing basis. Content is changed periodically, usually on the basis of a frequent needs assessment issued to the potential enrollees in the academy. The academy is structurally similar to the traditional university course as a form of inservice education, but this model has two important differences. First, the academy is an in-house effort sponsored by an educational agency specifically to address the needs of local practitioners. This is done without any reliance on another institution, such as a university. The academy also differs in that participation in its activities is client-driven. Involvement in academy activities normally comes from an individual's personal motivation and desire to learn and grow professionally, not solely from a need to meet requirements for continued certification by a state department of education, or to address the demands of some institution of higher education and its graduate-level degree programs.

We describe the academy structurally as a blend of the traditional university course and the locally sponsored institute that focuses directly on practitioners' concerns and interests. Next, we look at some of the positive aspects of the academy and some of its more significant drawbacks.

Advantages of the Academy

One major advantage of the inservice academy is found in its permanent structure, which has been established to address the continuing needs of practitioners. The academy typically offers a degree of stability that is seldom available in other approaches to inservice education, such as the institute. Most academies have a regular faculty made up of school district personnel or others, such as local university faculty members serving as consultants. These individuals can be counted on to return repeatedly to teach inservice classes. Institutes are often sponsored by national organizations or by entrepreneurs. As a result, they often lack permanence and stability.

A second advantage of the academy is that it is usually controlled directly by the practitioners who serve as participants. This feature distinguishes the academy from all of the other models reviewed in this book. Given the fact that the curriculum of the academy is most often established following an initial survey of practitioners' needs in the state or school district where the academy is established, there tends to be clear and immediate relevance to local needs.

The academy is best described as a type of grass-roots approach to inservice education, where participants are given considerable opportunity to influence the content and approaches used as part of the learning activity.

Disadvantages of the Academy

Drawbacks to the use of this model include the fact that most of the instruction provided is through one-way communication, the same mode utilized in the other two models of inservice education delivery (i.e., the traditional university course and the institute). Further, the issue of who will lead the inservice activities is not always clear. Those who have been charged with the responsibility of leading the inservice program are often external consultants hired by a school district to deal with substantive topics offered as part of the curriculum of the academy. They are outsiders brought to the local setting. As a result, the "faculty" of many inservice academies are highly respected scholars and experts in their fields. Such speakers, however, often lack a genuine understanding of the context of the local organization that might be sponsoring the academy. Consequently, the provider of the inservice program may be someone who comes to the scene with little or no knowledge of the conditions and events present in an organization that may have led to the need for the inservice in the first place. Outsiders take control of the planning and implementation of learning experiences and programs; participants have little involvement in the planning process.

A final restriction on the academy's use as a model for the delivery of inservice education for school administrators is found in the ever-present danger that too much of the focus for learning in this approach may be directed toward addressing issues in the here and now, whereas little emphasis may be given to finding long-term solutions to what may be extremely complex educational and organizational problems. Without attention directed toward changing this condition, the academy model might become little more than a type of protracted institute, complete with all the shortcomings of that model.

As we think again about the characteristics of effective inservice education, we note that the academy model is neither totally ineffective nor perfect. For example, the academy is designed primarily as a way for school systems to develop strategies to meet localized learning needs. Also, academies usually feature a fairly high degree of involvement by participants in the planning, implementation, and evaluation of programs. The inservice academy, then, is based on participant needs. More often than not, learning activities that make up the curricula of most academies deliberately avoid reliance on lectures and other forms of one-way communication and, instead, emphasize high-level participant involvement activities to promote participant learning. The academy is an attempt to ensure a type of continuity in the instructional sequence that is not usually found in the short-duration, one-shot types of programs offered as part of most institutes. Another feature of academies consistent with good inservice education practices is that they are frequently the product of school systems' interest in professional development. As a result, one usually finds strong commitment in terms of resources made available by central office administrators and school boards. On the other hand, because of the extreme cost associated with planning and carrying out academies, the majority of school systems do not make commitments to this model.

Academies are also consistent with effective practice because they normally feature programs that are subject to measures of quality control, delivered by individuals who know their fields well enough to be considered experts. Academies are often described as effective because they emphasize methods that ensure that individual participants' needs, interests, and concerns are addressed as completely as possible. Finally, the academy model parallels effective inservice education practice because most agencies that sponsor this model demand ongoing evaluation.

The inservice academy model misses the mark regarding effective inservice practices in a few ways as well. For example, most academies use instructional techniques still based largely on one-way communication. There is not too much difference between the practices of the academy and those of the institute or the traditional university course, reviewed earlier. Furthermore, the question of who will lead the inservice learning experience is not always clear. Frequently, instructors used in academy sessions are external consultants hired by the sponsoring agencies to deal with the substantive topics that may be offered in the academy curriculum. This ensures that someone with a knowledge base is available. Such external consultants, however, often have little awareness of the specific context of the organization sponsoring the academy. Consequently, the provider of inservice is someone with little or no knowledge of the events and conditions present in an organization that have, in turn, led to the need for the inservice in the first place. When such outsiders take control of the planning and carrying out of inservice programs, participants are again left with little involvement in the process. This violates one of the widely accepted characteristics of effective inservice practice.

A final restriction on the academy is that, although there may be an attempt to ensure that academy course offerings are relevant to participants, the danger exists that the focus of the curriculum will always be on the here and now, with little emphasis placed on long-term solutions. The concern here is that the academy will represent little more than a protracted institute or workshop.

Examples of the Academy Model

Inservice academies are sponsored by a variety of educational agencies. Two frequent sponsors are state departments of education and larger local school systems. Examples of the former include the Maine Principals' Academy (Donaldson, 1982, 1987), the Maryland Professional Development Academy (Huddle, 1982), and the Georgia Academy of School Executives (National Institute of Education, 1982); examples of the latter include the Leadership Development Program of the Columbus, Ohio, Schools, and the Des Moines (Iowa) Public Schools' Administrative Academy (Wise, 1981). In the sections that follow, we explore the Maryland and Des Moines programs in somewhat greater detail.

Maryland Professional Development Academy

The Maryland Professional Development Academy is an intensive inservice education program designed to enhance the instructional leadership skills of administrators across the state. It is financed entirely by the Maryland Department of Education. There are three major assumptions that have guided the efforts of this program since its inception (Sanders, 1987, pp. 101–103):

1. The state department of education can provide some type of training and staff development that is more appropriate to its role than to that of other agencies, such as local school systems. This statewide focus addresses the need for equity among the state's school systems.
2. The academy is based on the belief that effective schools research can be used as its basis and that the findings of this research can be translated into ongoing staff development.
3. School-based administrators are the proper leaders of staff development for their schools. They exercise leadership over staff development needs in their schools in the same way that they make responsible judgments on curriculum, instruction, and organizational climate.

The state provides resources to support the academy in a number of ways. First, a small full-time academy staff is maintained to coordinate the work of the academy each year. Second, the costs associated with providing training for up to 230 of the state's 2,258 school administrators are assumed by the state. Finally, money has been available for the academy to offer as many as nine different short-term learning experiences each year to practicing administrators. "These institutes focus on imparting skills to increase administrators' abilities to improve teaching, to provide clinical supervision, or to build more effective and more democratic patterns of teamwork among staff members" (Sanders, 1987, p. 100). The structure of the academy permits the inclusion of many other topics that may become of particular importance in the lives of participants at different times.

Des Moines Administrative Academy

In 1980 the Des Mones, Iowa, Public Schools announced that they were creating an internal staff development program for their administrative personnel. The creation of this unit was based on two fundamental assumptions (Wise, 1981, pp. 70–71):

1. Expanded training programs for administrators are vital if the district is going to meet community needs and expectations.
2. The training program must help administrative staff members perform effectively on a day-to-day basis, as well as develop skills in coping with the unexpected.

In addition, the academy has been designed to support broader district goals and assumptions related to professional growth for its employees:

1. The school district has a basic responsibility for the professional growth of its employees.
2. All administrative training and development must be designed to help administrators cope with problems and improve their managerial skills in relation to the goals and objectives of the district and their schools.
3. School administrators want to be as efficient and effective as possible.
4. Active and full participation of administrators will result if appropriate topics are offered and competent leadership is provided.
5. Ongoing training is necessary if effective leadership is to be maintained in the district.

Participating administrators are asked to identify topics to be covered in the sessions offered as part of the academy. Regardless of the topics selected, however, a prescribed structure has been identified for use in all sessions. All learning activities must provide evidence that they have been designed to address the concepts of collaboration, peer leadership, a sound cognitive base, experiential activities, and the maintenance and reinforcement of newly acquired concepts and skills. In this way, it is believed that the academy will include more than a simple collection of independent activities.

The Des Moines experience has been directed toward the belief that ongoing learning by educational leaders is a way to ensure that schools will be as effective as possible. It has also been based on a strong belief that isolated and unconnected learning activities are not appropriate ways to increase the opportunities to continue to learn.

Summary

In this chapter, another generic model for the delivery of ongoing inservice education for school leaders—the academy—was presented. It was noted that many different agencies have been responsible for sponsoring academies, but the groups most often seen as those that take the initiative in this approach have been local school districts and state departments of education.

Major strengths and weaknesses of the academy model were noted, particularly as they relate to some of the characteristics of effective inservice education practices. The chapter concluded with brief descriptions of two approaches to inservice education academies, the Maryland Professional Development Academy and the Des Moines, Iowa, Administrative Academy.

The models for the delivery of inservice education for practicing school administrators reviewed to this point have unique features that suggest that there are some subtle differences that make some models more effective than others. They are similar, however, in that they share many of the same limitations regarding participant involvement in selecting activities and learning objectives. All of the models are limited by the type of one-way communication that serves as the prevailing approach. In the next chapter, we offer one additional model for inservice delivery that is vastly different from these strategies. As we will see, networking approaches offer an alternative to most existing and conventional approaches to administrator inservice.

References

Donaldson, Gordon. (1982). Rx for school leadership: The Maine Principals' Academy. *Phi Delta Kappan, 63,* 6:400.

Donaldson, Gordon. (1987, January). The Maine Principals' Academy. *NASSP Bulletin, 71,* 495:40–43.

Huddle, Gene. (1982). A Maryland program for the professional development of school principals. *Phi Delta Kappan, 63,* 6:402.

National Institute of Education. (1982). *NIE directory of inservice training programs for principals.* Washington, DC: Program on Educational Policy and Organization.

Sanders, A. Skipp. (1987). Maryland's MPDA: The Maryland Professional Development Academy and its odyssey in comprehensive training. In J. Murphy & P. Hallinger (Eds.), *Approaches to administrative training in education.* Albany: State University of New York Press.

Wise, James E. (1981, May). Staff development for administrators—An administrative academy. *Journal of Staff Development. 2,* 1:70–77.

CHAPTER FOURTEEN

Networking as a Form of Inservice

The final model for the delivery of inservice that we consider is *networking*. This approach involves linking individuals in different schools or districts for the purpose of sharing concerns and effective practices on an ongoing basis. There is a significant difference between this approach and the others reviewed in that, in networking, the primary responsibility for controlling the learning experience lies directly with the participants themselves and not with their professional associations, the state education agency, or some nearby university. Networks tend to be informal arrangements that emerge when administrators seek out colleagues who share similar concerns and potential solutions to problems.

In this chapter we examine the use of networking as an approach to providing ongoing support to practicing school administrators. We begin by considering some of the fundamental assumptions associated with the belief that collegiality is a desirable goal of inservice education for school leaders. Second, we look at some of the major strengths and advantages associated with networks. Next, we look at some major disadvantages. Finally, we present two existing approaches to administrator inservice that are based on the networking model.

Assumptions of Collegiality

Recent suggestions that networking should be used for professional development of school administrators seem to be based largely on the belief that collegial support arrangements are needed. When educators are able to form linkage relationships with one another, good things happen. Recent descriptions of effective organizations

161

suggest that, when norms of mutual support and collegiality are present, those organizations are likely to be sustained over longer periods of time.

Research related to the needs of beginning school administrators also supports the view that collegiality should be fostered. Studies by Daresh (1986) and Weindling and Earley (1987) indicate that school administrators tend to lead lives that are largely isolated from their peers. As a result, efforts to bring people together in some meaningful way are highly prized. It is not surprising, then, that networks of school administrators have been increasingly recognized as successful approaches to providing for the delivery of inservice education experiences.

There is an important difference between simply bringing administrators together periodically and developing true collegial relationships. In the former case, no clear goals are present to guide the bringing together of different individuals. As a result, no sharing or open communication takes place. Further, people are not together to achieve common, shared goals. In true collegial relationships, there is a focused objective toward which individuals are directed, and the common pursuit of this objective forms the bond between and among members of the collegial group. As a result, there is a great difference between a bunch of school principals who happen to get together periodically for social occasions, and a group of administrators who gather on a regular basis to engage in activities that have been deliberately planned as a way to encourage collective movement toward enhanced professional performance.

Advantages of Networking

In terms of what we noted earlier about the desirable characteristics of effective inservice learning experiences—that is, using peer interaction among professionals, avoiding standardized inservice "packages," utilizing participant input in the establishment of inservice objectives and activities, and so forth—networking offers many advantages over the other inservice approaches and models of inservice examined earlier. Networking holds that individuals who share common problems are able to come together periodically to gain support from colleagues and also to gain additional insights and support from others who face similar problems. The focus in networking is definitely on multidirectional communication and participant involvement. No one plays the role of teacher in networking. The topics addressed come directly from the concerns of participants, not from a professor or workshop designer who does not necessarily know who will be enrolled in the course or the workshop. Finally, networking encourages and is built on the premise that long-term relationships among inservice participants are desirable. As a result, this approach to inservice education is different from the kind of isolated learning that goes on in the institute, the traditional university course, or the inservice academy.

If administrators' perceptions of the desirability of different models of inservice delivery are any indication of the potential effectiveness of a model, then networking should be viewed as a very successful approach.

Disadvantages of Networking

Networking also has some disadvantages. It is not unusual for the common interest groups that come together to form networks, ostensibly to deal with school-related concerns, to lose their focus and become social gatherings more than professional gatherings. Although the meeting of a group engaged in networking should not necessarily be as formal as the meeting of a corporate board, it should focus on professional issues and not serve solely or even primarily as a party for participants.

Another problem with networking is that, although this arrangement is rooted in informality and the sharing of common concerns, there is a tendency for networks to become so informal and loose-knit that members freely drop in and out of the group. Often there is no long-term commitment to the network group or to its goals as instruments of ongoing professional development.

Finally, although an advantage of networking can be the fact that no one controls the group while acting in the role of teacher, problems can result when responsibility for directing the group is totally ignored. Although participant involvement in inservice planning and implementation is unquestionably a key ingredient for effectiveness, someone must still lead.

Examples of Networking Arrangements

In this section, we provide two examples of structured learning experiences for administrator inservice that are based on the assumption that a powerful technique for encouraging professional growth is the formation of collegial support networks for practicing school administrators. These two programs are the Principals' Inservice Program and Project Leadership.

Principals' Inservice Program

This program, developed with support from the Institute for Development of Educational Activities, Inc. (/I/D/E/A/), represents an attempt to develop effective administrator inservice by focusing directly and exclusively on the local school situation and the needs of local principals as participants. An inherent assumption is that principals need a way to learn how to be better by using their present knowledge and their own awareness of their needs as a starting point for professional development.

The structure used to enable principals to learn how to use their present knowledge to improve their performance consists of collegial support groups, each including six to ten principals. These groups enable principals to work together to practice the behaviors that enable them to work on long- and short-term problems and also to critique openly and honestly their efforts to improve themselves and their schools. Through collegial support groups, individuals can bring their problems to others and, while following a tightly defined agenda of planned learning activities, can share their successes with persons who understand and appreciate the role of the principal.

The Principals' Inservice Program was piloted in 1978–1979 with groups of rural, suburban, and urban principals and was then introduced to school districts across the nation as more specially trained group facilitators became available. The program has now expanded to include 145 facilitators leading collegial support groups with more than 1,500 principals from 25 states and three foreign countries (LaPlant, 1987).

The commitment made by principals who wish to follow the program is to participate in day-long meetings of the collegial support group once each month over at least a two-year period. Four objectives serve as the focus of the monthly sessions, which are directed by the facilitator:

1. Each principal, as a member of a collegial support group, designs, implements, and evaluates a plan to increase his or her leadership capability.

2. Each principal designs, implements, and evaluates a school improvement project that involves the staff in addressing an identified need within the school.
3. Members of the collegial support group provide assistance and encouragement to one another in professional development and school improvement efforts.
4. Each principal adopts the search for continuous improvement as a guiding principle and accepts personal responsibility for his or her role in the improvement process.

The Principals' Inservice Program is based on the belief that there are many excellent principals who are talented, committed, and willing to devote energy to improving their own performance and their schools' programs. They want to exercise their role as the educational leader of their schools. The reasons that many principals do not achieve their goals, however, are found in the isolation of the role, complete with the frequently heard complaints that principals lack time and are faced with so many nagging daily problems that real professional growth is impossible. Principals rarely have the opportunity to express their concerns and frustrations to other principals who can understand their problems without also judging the performance of their colleagues.

The strength of the Principals' Inservice Program lies in the fact that it enables principals to engage in continuous self-improvement and professional growth. It represents an effort to make the individual principal responsible for his or her own learning and development. In short, the principal truly becomes the "number one learner" who can serve as a powerful role model to students and staff in his or her school.

Project Leadership

In 1981 the Association of California School Administrators introduced an inservice program that has as its primary goal the linkage of practicing school administrators in support networks for the purpose of sharing concerns related to their daily jobs. This model is called Project Leadership (Kipp, Thayer, & Olivero, 1981), and it relies on the ability of school administrators to learn from each other through the sharing of oral tradition (Orlich, 1989). A critical difference between this approach and the Principals' Inservice Program is that Project Leadership is based on the assumption that groups that are brought together to form collegial networks do not necessarily have to represent only one particular administrative role, such as principal. In this approach, central office administrators can be mixed with building-level leaders in the same groups.

The stated goals of Project Leadership are as follows:

1. To provide administrators with an opportunity for both initial and renewal education in essential basic skills.
2. To provide districts with leaders who can educate other administrators within the district.
3. To provide individually selected options for the improvement of personal skills or skills to meet the needs of other administrators in the district.
4. To create a climate for learning that offers planned procedures for attaining high-priority goals, particularly goals in areas that will enhance the administrator's impact on teachers and students.
5. To create a collegial sense among participants.
6. To review relevant research and successful practices for possible transfer to Project Leadership participants.
7. To disseminate the latest concepts and successful programs in school management and curriculum leadership.
8. To provide field-tested learning materials for participants to use in their districts (Orlich, 1989, pp. 133–134).

Project Leadership is a program disseminated through the state affiliates of professional associations of school administrators. These groups take primary responsibility for disseminating and coordinating the project among interested groups of administrators. Structurally, the state associations form regional groupings of administrators as Satellite Groups, each of which is led by a practicing school administrator.

A unique feature of Project Leadership is the fact that all participants in a state are brought together at least once each year for statewide meetings. During these sessions, issues identified as common concerns of all local participants are discussed. In addition, the statements of goals and objectives articulated by participating administrators are shared, and support is sought for the attainment of stated improvement plans.

"Project Leadership activities allow each participant to become a human resource. The training network [established through statewide coordination efforts] maintains the oral tradition. Individuals can easily call any network member for help or information. Further, local school districts develop the potential for additional inservice projects at almost no cost" (Orlich, 1989, p. 134). There is a strong emphasis on the ability of the individual school administrator to form positive links with colleagues while also pursuing the goal of maintaining the importance of instructional priorities in the school or district.

Summary

The final structured model for the delivery of inservice education for school administrators was reviewed in this chapter. We described this model as networking, and it is based on the fundamental belief that collegial relationships may be used to enhance the opportunities to engage in personal and professional growth.

We began with a brief review of some of the major assumptions associated with the development of collegiality as a desirable goal for administrator professional development. We noted, in particular, that there is a consistent need for strategies to be discovered that will reduce the sense of alienation and isolation so often associated with leadership roles. Next, we considered the major advantages and disadvantages associated with networking. Finally, we looked at two examples of networking, the Principals' Inservice Program and Project Leadership.

References

Daresh, John C. (1986, Summer). Support for beginning principals: First hurdles are highest. *Theory into Practice, 25,* 3: 168–173.

Kipp, William, Thayer, Arthur N., & Olivero, James L. (1981). *Project Leadership—Introductory component.* Newport Beach: Association of California School Administrators.

LaPlant, James C. (1987). Facilitating /I/D/E/A/ principals' collegial support groups as a means of professional development and school improvement. In J. Murphy & P. Hallinger (Eds.), *Approaches to administrative training in education.* Albany: State University of New York Press.

Orlich, Donald C. (1989). *Staff development: Enhancing human potential.* Boston: Allyn and Bacon.

Weindling, Dick, & Earley, Peter. (1987). *The secondary headship: The first years.* Philadelphia: NFER-Nelson.

CHAPTER FIFTEEN

Emerging Trends, Promising Practices

Throughout this book, we have examined a wide variety of issues associated with the professional development of school administrators. As a backdrop to this examination, we have provided an argument that such development is central to the creation of more successful schools because leadership is a vital part of more effective educational practice.

Our review began with the presentation of a tridimensional model of professional development, which suggested that effective practice is based on program planning that includes learning experiences that provide for opportunities for field-based activities, academic experiences, and attention to personal and professional formation. We also proposed a definition of professional development that includes the phases of preservice preparation, initial professional induction, and ongoing inservice education. We noted that the tridimensional model's components must be included as part of all three of these phases of professional development. As we considered the various aspects of the preparation of educational leaders and later support for them in practice, we provided descriptions of existing effective practices sponsored by universities, professional associations of school administrators, local school districts, and state departments of education.

In this final chapter we suggest some of the future trends that are likely to be seen in the area of educational leadership and that will have important implications for professional development. We also present a few examples of what we consider promising practices and programs in the areas of preservice preparation, induction, and ongoing inservice education.

Professional Development Trends

Our analysis of the current scene in the area of professional development for school administrators suggests five important issues that will need to be addressed in the next few years.

> *1. Efforts will continue to find ways to make the field of educational administration more inclusive and representative.*

Two factors will contribute to this trend. First, demographic data consistently show that the United States is quickly moving toward a population in which former ethnic and racial minorities together will constitute the majority, particularly in urban areas, the Southwest, and the Southeast. Thus, there is an expectation that school leaders will increasingly come from the ranks of African Americans, Asians, and Hispanics in order that school personnel may more accurately reflect the backgrounds and characteristics of student populations. The result of this search for greater representativeness, we believe, will cause school systems to press for more applicants for leadership roles who come from groups traditionally underrepresented in school administrative offices.

Second, there is growing recognition that large segments of society have long been excluded from significant professional roles. School administrators, as a group, tend to be white, Anglo, and male. In the future, we believe, efforts will be increased to ensure that greater numbers of school principals, superintendents, and other administrators will not come from these traditional majority groups, if for no other reason than to make certain that a greater percentage of individuals in this nation are included in critical societal roles.

Implications for professional development are clear. At the preservice phase, efforts need to be increased to find ways to identify, recruit, and select greater numbers of individuals from populations traditionally not included in educational leadership. Induction programs need to be developed to increase the likelihood that, once individuals are recruited to leadership roles, they are provided with conditions that increase the likelihood that they will succeed. Finally, special forms of ongoing inservice education are needed to provide continuing supportive arrangements.

2. Direct legislative influence will continue to grow in the area of educational policy development.

The good news is that schools have been discovered by political figures in recent years. And the bad (or at least questionable) news is that schools have been discovered by political figures. We believe that this condition will continue well into the future and will also play a central role in the world of administrator professional development.

One way in which this discovery by politicians will become apparent is through greater attention to the role of the school principal as the object of both great criticism and great appreciation. In the former case, public pronouncements regarding the inefficacy of public education are including more references to administrative behavior by principals as a barrier to creative, dynamic, and supposedly more educationally effective practice by schoolteachers, students, and parents. In the latter case, the political dialogue seems increasingly committed to a recognition that principals and other educational administrators hold the key to providing the type of school-based leadership that is so vital to the enhancement of the teaching and learning process.

The outcome of this increased interest in educational leadership by the body politic is that more legislative action now centers on ways of improving (if not deliberately stated as "reforming") the business of educational leadership. As examples of this, legislatively mandated, comprehensive educational reform packages have recently been put into effect in North Carolina and Maine, and such legislation is pending in Colorado and Ohio. Reforms have looked at the ways in which school administrators are initially prepared (North Carolina), first brought into their roles (Ohio), and provided with opportunities for focused professional development (Maine and Colorado). Such efforts to attend to the needs of school administrators are likely to increase in frequency and detail throughout the foreseeable future.

3. Greater attention will be directed to alliances between public education and private industry.

The result of linkages between school systems and the corporate world will be an increasingly popular phenomenon in years to come, and many of these relationships will focus on the enhancement of the role of educational administrators. The leaders of private corporations are becoming more assertive and vocal in expressing their displeasure at what they believe is going on in the nation's public schools. Not surprisingly, these individuals quickly associate the lack of productivity—defined normally as low scores on standardized achievement tests and the lack of basic communication and computation skills in the labor force—with the lack of effective management. U.S. corporations succeed or fail on the basis of behaviors in board rooms and executive suites; U.S. schools are in trouble because of what is not taking place in the actions of school boards and school administrators.

Efforts by private corporations to intervene directly in the improvement of administrative practices in schools are seen frequently. One example of such an effort is seen in the work of IBM to promote regional training activities designed to make practicing school principals more sensitive in regarding students, parents, and their local communities as "clients" or "customers" of the public education "enterprise," rather than as members of a type of captive audience that must accept whatever product the public school systems offer. This type of effort is criticized by many educators as a form of tampering with the traditional domain of professionals. Further, depictions of students as clients, parents as customers, teachers as producers, and administrators as corporate executives might be little more than the use of new bottles to house the old wine of jargon from the scientific management era, as described in Chapter 1. It makes little sense, however, to engage in a prolonged debate over this matter. Private industry will continue to emerge as an increasingly potent player in efforts to reform education in this country. When this is coupled with the increased political attention that will be directed toward the schools of the future, it would be naive to assume anything but more attention to emerging relationships involving public schools and private corporations.

This observation has many implications for the improvement of administrator professional development. Whether we are talking about preservice, induction, or inservice applications, program designers must pay consistent attention to the ways in which private corporations might become involved in either planning or actually providing training. In addition, it is crucial that aspiring as well as practicing school administrators engage in conversations with private industry so that school personnel will be aware of the perceptions of other influential actors in the public sector.

**4. Expectations will continue to rise regarding the need
to try dramatically new practices in public schools.**

From the perspectives of private industry, political figures,
and the mass media, at least, schools cannot guard the status quo for
the future. The polite academic discussions of school reform from the
1970s and early 1980s have now become loud calls for complete
restructuring of education. Expectations that school districts would
find ways to promote competitive options through the exercise of
"schools of choice" proposals are not mild suggestions. Rather, a
large percentage of the public now believes that schools must
change, and change quickly and radically.

This image, of course, has a direct and immediate impact on
the educational administrator. The traditional image of the superintendent or principal as the guardian of local norms and traditional
practices will shift to expectations that creativity and risk-taking
behaviors will become more common. Professional development
opportunities will thus play a critical role in helping administrators
who have faithfully "kept the ship afloat" acquire skills more consistent with sometimes "rocking the boat."

**5. The business of schools will increasingly become
defined as the promotion of human resource development.**

We are convinced that future educational improvement will be
measured by such things as the extent to which students express
more positive self-images and feelings of personal worth and accomplishment. Such measures will also be applied to the desired perceptions of teachers and others who work in schools. We think that
the future holds the likelihood that schools will need to become less
the sites of *teaching* than they are environments for *learning*.

The implications for school administrators of such a
transformation are great. Many who serve as educational leaders
see their roles as promoters of overall organizational efficiency. The
future suggests that principals and superintendents will need to
learn skills and behaviors more consistent with the roles of
architects and sculptors who strive to create internal organizational cultures and climates that are learning environments, not
teaching factories. Administrators will need to learn more about
the essence of teacher empowerment, rather than simply developing
the ability to mouth slogans and agree that this is, indeed, a "good
idea."

These observations of future trends are not meant to serve as an exhaustive list of magical predictions. Instead, we have made a few comments regarding some major issues that we believe will have an impact on the nature of the school administrator's role in the future. With these broad predictions, we also expect that behaviors and attitudes will need to change sufficiently to warrant even more attention to the discovery of programs and practices available to school leaders at each of the three stages of professional development—preservice preparation, induction, and ongoing inservice education. In the next section, we look at some promising strategies that are emerging or, in some cases, already well established.

Promising Practices

We see some examples of encouraging practices associated with preservice preparation activities, initial induction, and continuing inservice.

Promising Preservice Practices

In our discussions earlier in this book, we noted both great hope and despair concerning the nature of existing preservice programs for aspiring school administrators. In our discussion of academic preparation in Chapter 2, for example, we provided descriptions of current efforts to promote reform at such institutions as the University of Northern Colorado, the State University of New York at Buffalo, and The Ohio State University. By contrast, when we looked at the nature of traditional university courses as a form of delivery for administrator inservice in Chapter 11, we noted that the structural elements of most existing programs still rely largely on one-way communication of professor-controlled information. Despite any changes to preservice programs, and in addition to some of the programs that now go beyond the status quo, we have found at least two additional efforts that hold promise in the areas of improving preparatory programs.

Danforth Principals' Preparation Program
In 1986 the Danforth Foundation of St. Louis announced a major new funding initiative which had as its long-term goal the

improvement of university-based programs that have been designed to prepare individuals to assume school principalships. Beyond that goal, the Danforth Principal Preparation Program has three additional continuing objectives:

1. To promote the development of collaborative relationships between selected universities and neighboring school systems, with regard to the preservice preparation of future school principals.
2. To enable planners of innovative preservice principal preparation programs to take risks and develop learning activities that allow future school principals to engage in experiential learning activities.
3. To provide support to programs that would address the need to encourage women and minorities, as representatives of populations traditionally underrepresented in school leadership roles, to pursue careers in the principalship.

The foundation prescribed no particular structure for the designers of innovative programs, with the exception that they were expected to adhere to the goal and objectives just noted. There have been similarities among the different programs that have developed as a result of the Danforth support. For example, all programs have made use of collaborative learning arrangements so that aspiring principals could be brought together to form learning teams, or cohorts. Another structural element common to all Danforth programs across the nation has been reliance on mentoring relationships formed between Danforth candidates and practicing school administrators from local school systems.

Beginning with three institutions during the 1987–1988 academic year (the University of Alabama, Georgia State University, and The Ohio State University), a small group of institutions have been invited to participate in this effort through the receipt of relatively small (approximately $40,000), nonrenewable grants from the foundation. At present, five cycles of the program, comprising 24 institutions, have been initiated. More than 300 aspiring school leaders, or "Danforth candidates," have completed programs across the nation.

Those who have looked into the outcomes of the foundation's efforts have begun to recognize certain benefits. First, Danforth candidates have had a much clearer chance to witness the realities of practice in educational administration. Second, people who participated in Danforth have indicated that their leadership preparation experiences have focused very directly on their ability to become more personally reflective regarding the nature of educational administration. Third, people have indicated that they believed they were better acquainted with many of the technical skills required of school administrators. Finally, in a somewhat surprising finding, Marsha Playko (1991) discovered that at least some Danforth candidates, after having participated in Danforth programs, concluded that they were no longer interested in formal careers as educational administrators. Instead, they identified different routes to the fulfillment of their leadership goals in schools.

The Danforth Principal Preparation Program has not been a panacea. There is no suggestion that participation in this type of program will automatically or necessarily guarantee any kind of long-term effectiveness on the job. And no one can yet claim that schools are necessarily more effective when principals have served earlier as Danforth candidates. Nevertheless, those who have observed the progress of Danforth programs across the nation have noted that these activities have started to demonstrate some positive effects on the nature of preservice preparation programs for school leaders.

Assessment Centers

Another effort to make some modifications in the practices associated with the preservice preparation of school administrators has involved the application of assessment center methodology, either as an initial screening technique designed to ensure that only individuals with clearly identified abilities are permitted to participate in preparatory activities, or as a way to guide individuals in the pursuit of specific, identified leadership skills. Assessment centers used as part of leadership development are not new. During World War II, the U.S. Army developed techniques designed to ascertain the likelihood that certain individuals would be more or less likely to succeed in performing tasks while in the service. After the war, a number of private corporations—most notably AT&T—made modifications in the basic army assessment techniques so that they would be able to provide screening exercises to identify individuals who possessed the requisite knowledge, attitudes, values, and skills that would likely make them effective corporate managers.

Assessment centers are examples of what we have also called "competency-based approaches to administrator training" (Daresh & LaPlant, 1984). A widely known model is the Assessment Center of the National Association of Secondary School Principals (NASSP)

(Schmitt, 1980), which holds that persons possessing skills in problem analysis, judgment, organizational ability, decisiveness, leadership, sensitivity, range of interests, personal motivation, stress tolerance, values clarification, and oral and written communication skills make the best candidates for administrative positions. Another effort is the set of administrator preparation guidelines set forth by the American Association of School Administrators (AASA) (Hoyle, 1983). These guidelines suggest that administrators need to be skillful in improving school climate, understanding the politics of schooling, managing instruction, developing curriculum, designing inservice, planning for effective resource use, and conducting research.

What is intriguing about this form of professional development is that assessment center programs have been suggested as ways to determine the precise skills necessary for effective administration. It is assumed that when skills are identified, people can be prepared to attain those skills. Competency-based programs offer aspiring administrators the chance to work toward professional development in a more focused way than through the traditional university course alone.

There are also some drawbacks to the use of assessment center techniques. For one thing, competency frameworks have the tendency to create situations where "recipes for effectiveness" are suggested. That is, if an aspiring administrator completes a series of prescribed tasks, he or she will be an "effective" school leader. Another limitation is the availability of appropriate training processes and expertise to deliver all targeted competencies. Who would lead future administrators toward learning stress tolerance, sensitivity, or any other named skill?

Despite any shortcomings to the use of assessment centers as part of preservice preparation, we emphasize that this approach has potential for providing a framework to help those who lead the preparation programs as well as those who are involved as students of administration.

Induction Programs

There are also some developments taking place in programs that are available to support beginning administrators.

The Ohio Entry-Year Program

The certification standards for teachers and all other educational personnel in Ohio require that all people hired by school systems must be provided with a planned program of learning experiences in their first year of employment. It is believed that these experiences will increase the likelihood that the newly hired individuals will achieve some degree of success. Seven components are included in the Entry-Year Standard:

1. A statement of assurances must be signed by the superintendent and filed with the state department indicating that the district has complied with the standard.
2. A description of the entry-year program shall be on file at the office of the superintendent.
3. A method for providing specific orientation to school system expectations and practices must be developed.
4. A process for identifying training, and assigning mentors must be prepared.
5. A statement of how the local entry-year program fits a larger effort to enhance ongoing professional development must be made.
6. A strategy of self-evaluation of the program at the district level must be implemented.
7. Participation in a formal state evaluation of the program every five years must take place.

The Entry-Year Standard has grown from a need perceived by practitioners across the state of Ohio who worked with the state department to design approaches to helping beginning colleagues. The features of the Entry-Year Program reflect the concerns of school personnel who want to see educational improvement through the improvement of leaders.

Part of the standard calls for the designation of experienced administrators to serve as mentors to beginning school administrators. Mentors should be provided with sufficient training to enable them to carry out their duties.

No single "entry-year model" has been mandated for adoption across Ohio. Beginning administrators encounter unique problems on the job. School systems are expected to look at their own needs, characteristics, and priorities in order to devise programs that fit the needs of their particular districts.

Beaverton, Oregon, Induction Process

The Beaverton, Oregon, school district is a suburban system outside of Portland. It enrolls nearly 25,000 students. In the mid-

1980s; it began a special principal preparation program as a way to find qualified individuals to step into assistant principal and principal positions that were expected to open up as a result of a large number of retirements anticipated into the 1990s. As the preservice preparation program began to yield more and more individuals who assumed administrator roles, another program was initiated to support many new administrators.

One part of the Beaverton Induction Process is directed toward providing orientation to the school district. Beginners are linked with the central office to learn how things are done in Beaverton. New principals are able to meet with their immediate district-level supervisors for at least one hour every two weeks. "During the meetings, central office administrators give rookies detailed instruction on various aspects of their jobs such as teacher evaluations and budgeting. Orientations, therefore, do not occur all at once, but instead are spread out over the year so as not to overload rookie administrators" (Anderson, 1988, p. 36).

A second dimension of the Beaverton program deals with orientation to individual school buildings. One-to-one interviews are arranged between the new principal and the individual that he or she is replacing. In addition, the district personnel director spends time with each new principal to give him or her a thorough overview of each staff member, including potential problems.

The third way in which new administrators are provided with structured entry-level support is through a district-sponsored support network for beginning principals. This networking is an informal arrangement wherein experienced principals make it a regular part of their work to go to lunch or otherwise visit with different newcomers at least twice each month.

The Beaverton Induction Process has had two benefits. First, it is a system that is responsive to the unique difficulties that are typically faced by most beginning school administrators. Further, the program has systemic benefits because it ensures that new principals are likely to become productive members of the district leadership team much more quickly than they might if they were simply allowed to find their own way into the system.

Inservice Education Programs

We include three relatively recent programs that we believe represent significant additions to the field of inservice education available for school administrators. These three programs are Peer-Assisted Leadership, the APEX Program for Reflective Principals, and principals' centers.

Peer-Assisted Leadership

In 1983, the Project on Instructional Management at the Far West Regional Educational Laboratory in San Francisco incorporated the findings of its work on instructional leadership behavior into a program designed to provide ongoing support and inservice learning opportunities to practicing school administrators. This program, Peer-Assisted Leadership (PAL), is currently being implemented with numerous groups of administrators across the nation.

PAL works by pairing principals with peers to conduct structured shadowing along with intensive reflective interviewing. After these have taken place, peer groups meet to confer, analyze, and synthesize the findings derived from their interviewing and shadowing activities. Through this method, colleagues are brought together in a way that enables them to share insights regarding instructional leadership strategies out in the field.

Barnett (1987) identified five goals for principals who participate in PAL:

1. Learn and apply new ways to think about instructional leadership.
2. Analyze their own and another principal's behavior.
3. Integrate the instructional leadership behavior derived from their field-based observations into their own settings.
4. Learn how other principals lead their schools.
5. Form a collegial support system in which new ideas and insights are shared and change is nurtured and supported.

At least four major benefits have been derived by individuals participating in PAL. First, the program allows for more reflective and introspective behavior on the part of principals. This valuable activity is often found to be something not normally enjoyed by most practitioners (Barnett, 1987). Second, the program exposes principals to many new practices as they see what is taking place in other schools and districts. Third, PAL has been identified as a powerful way to reduce the sense of isolation felt by school administrators. Finally, those who have participated in PAL have indicated that they often realized that their involvement frequently served as a visible indication to their faculties that peer relationships were highly desirable. In short, they served as authentic role models for teachers, who typically gained much from increased interaction with their peers as well.

APEX Center for Reflective Practice

In 1984 Paula Silver began the Center for Advancing Principalship Excellence (APEX) at the University of Illinois–Urbana. The primary purpose of this center was to encourage practicing principals to engage in reflection on the nature of their job responsibilities and the problems associated with those duties. In turn, principals are expected to develop formal descriptions of the critical incidents that they face on the job each day as case records, which may in turn be shared with colleagues. The ultimate goal of this reflective sharing process among administrators is not necessarily to solve all problems. Rather, there is an assumption that people who share experiences will be able to gain important insights about themselves and their schools by having made their thoughts and actions explicit in the statement of case records (Silver, 1986).

Since the death of its founder, the APEX Center has been relocated to Hofstra University. At present, it is operated as a joint venture of Hofstra and the University Council for Educational Administration, as well as individual administrators who serve as paid members. The original vision of using practitioners' own recollections of significant administrative issues as the basis for developing greater reflection on practice has been maintained. It is likely that the concept of sharing case records to improve administrative practice will continue to be developed in the next few years.

Principals' Centers

The final promising inservice practice that we mention is the use of regional principals' centers as a way to promote greater opportunities for practicing administrators to share their concerns with colleagues. Further, principals' centers are mechanisms that promote the development of skills by practitioners to take greater control over their own learning and professional development.

David Erlandson (1987) noted the following about this strategy for administrator professional development:

> *Principals' centers cannot supplant, nor even compete with, the agencies and associations that have traditionally supported principals. They are in the business of fostering renewal*

> *through relationships designed to continue only so long as they*
> *fulfill needs unmet by other groups. When other groups meet*
> *these needs, principals' centers will blend with them and seek*
> *new roles. Principals' centers have only their new energy and*
> *promise to offer; structurally, they cannot compete with more*
> *mature organizations. (p. 1)*

At present there are more than a hundred institutions operating across the nation that take on the characteristics of what we are calling principals' centers. They are associated with a variety of different organizations—universities, state departments of education, and individual school districts. Perhaps the oldest center has been the one located at Harvard University, which began its work in 1981 (Van Der Bogert, 1987). With the assistance of the Danforth Foundation, Roland Barth, the founder of the Harvard Center, worked to develop a National Network of Principals' Center to encourage open dialogue among those who lead similar efforts. Each year, a nationwide "Principals' Center Conversation" brings together center leaders, principals, and others interested in the improvement of this strategy.

There is some suggestion that the center movement across the nation has started to lose some of its momentum in recent years. If this is true, we are concerned because the centers have represented a very effective way to ensure that the professional development of school leaders receives the attention it deserves.

Summary

We have suggested that the professional development of school administrators is an important issue to be addressed by school systems interested in improving practice. Any system of professional development must deal with three distinct developmental phases: preservice preparation, induction, and ongoing inservice education.

In this final chapter, we returned to these three phases and indicated that there are certain emerging programs and effective practices that have great promise related to the improvement of professional development programs for school administrators. We presented information concerning programs such as the APEX Center at Hofstra University, Peer-Assisted Leadership, and principals' centers. We framed our discussion of these programs by first noting that there are certain trends related to administrator development that are likely to persist in the immediate future. We noted that these trends are not passing fads; they deal with the core values of administration of schools. As a result, they must be taken into account by those who would deal responsibly with learning experiences for school leaders.

We conclude this book by returning to a point that we raised in the opening pages. We believe that school administrators are important people who have a tremendous impact on the quality of life for students, parents, teachers, and communities in general. We also believe that these important people merit attention by those who would have the formal or informal duty of providing for their ability to learn more about children, communities, learning, environments, and other issues that have an impact on what goes on in schools and what makes for better learning. Professional development for school administrators is not simply a stylish activity. It is a vital necessity.

References

Anderson, Mark. (1989). *Induction programs for principals*. Project paper of the Oregon School Study Council. Eugene: University of Oregon.

Barnett, Bruce G. (1985). Peer-assisted leadership: Peer observation and feedback as catalysts for professional growth. In J. Murphy & P. Hallinger (Eds.), *Approaches to administrative training in education*. Albany: State University of New York Press.

Erlandson, David. (1987). Principals' centers: Diversity reflects strength of concept. *NASSP Bulletin, 71,* 495:1.

Hoyle, John. (1983). *Guidelines for the preparation of school administrators*. Arlington, VA: American Association of School Administrators.

Playko, Marsha A. (1991). *The voyage to leadership: Journeys of four teachers*. Unpublished Ph.D. dissertation, The Ohio State University.

Schmitt, N. (1980). Validation of the NASSP Assessment Center: An overview and some preliminary findings. *NASSP Bulletin, 64,* 438:107–118.

Silver, Paul F. (1986). Case records: A reflective practice approach to administrator development. *Theory into Practice, 25,* 3:161–167.

Van Der Bogert, Rebecca. (1987). The growth of principals' centers. *NASSP Bulletin, 71,* 495:3–4.

Index